directions

new FOR
CONTINUING
EDUCATION

number 3 • 1979

new directions for continuing education

a quarterly sourcebook
Alan B. Knox, Editor-in-Chief

number 3, 1979

assessing the impact of continuing education

alan b. knox
guest editor

Jossey-Bass Inc., Publishers
San Francisco • Washington • London

ASSESSING THE IMPACT OF CONTINUING EDUCATION
New Directions for Continuing Education
Number 3, 1979
    Alan B. Knox, Guest Editor

New Directions for Continuing Education is published quarterly
by Jossey-Bass Inc., Publishers. Subscriptions are available
at the regular rate for institutions, libraries, and agencies
of $25 for one year. Individuals may subscribe at the special
professional rate of $15 for one year. Application to mail at
second-class postage rates is pending at San Francisco, California,
and at additional mailing offices.

Correspondence:
Subscriptions, single-issue orders, change of address notices,
undelivered copies, and other correspondence should be sent to
New Directions Subscriptions, Jossey-Bass Inc., Publishers,
433 California Street, San Francisco, California 94104.
Editorial correspondence should be sent to the Editor-in-Chief,
Alan B. Knox, Office for the Study of Continuing Professional
Education, University of Illinois at Urbana-Champaign,
Urbana, Illinois 61801.

Library of Congress Catalogue Card Number LC 79-89532

Cover design by Willi Baum
Manufactured in the United States of America

contents

(Further sources and readings can be found at the end of each chapter.)

editor's notes

Program improvement and justification are important tasks of continuing education practitioners. Over the years, practitioners have given substantial attention to informal evaluation procedures for program improvement. However, growing visibility and expectations regarding continuing education of adults are increasing the importance of assessing the impact of continuing education. Evaluating the impact of education means going beyond measures of satisfaction and learning gain, to assessment of practical application in terms of changed performance and societal benefits. The purposes of this sourcebook are to explore reasons why evaluation of impact is important, to describe procedures for impact evaluation in various segments of the field, to summarize findings regarding the impact of continuing education, to identify concepts and literature useful to those who conduct impact evaluation, and to suggest desirable and feasible approaches to future impact evaluation studies.

Most of the chapters report on experience with impact evaluation in a segment of the field such as schools, universities, employers, or professional associations. These chapters typically indicate evaluation settings, purposes, procedures, findings, and uses. The introductory chapter provides a rationale for continuing education impact evaluation and reports on impact evaluations not covered in the subsequent chapters. The rest of the chapters deal with issues in planning and conducting impact evaluations. Such issues include building practitioner expertise to conduct evaluation studies, making evaluation projects cost-effective, using concepts and materials from the general field of educational evaluation, and using what we now know to conduct more beneficial impact evaluation studies in the future.

Alan B. Knox
Editor

An overview of impact evaluation issues, approaches, and studies provides a general framework for this sourcebook and indicates the types of impact studies that have been conducted.

what difference does it make?

alan b. knox

Continuing education practitioners judge their programs in order to improve and justify them in ways that are focused and manageable. Practitioners have long used informal evaluation procedures in an effort to improve the educational process. Examples include participant reaction forms and analysis of trends in enrollments and attrition. Efforts to assess the impact of continuing education have been more rare. This sourcebook provides a rationale and examples of impact evaluations to help practitioners select and use procedures to assess and justify the benefits of their programs to participants and society. The early sections of the chapter present an approach to impact evaluation. The remainder contains illustrative summaries of impact studies from throughout the field of continuing education.

evaluation of process and outcomes

Useful program evaluation is an integral part of the program development process. As such, the benefits of such evaluation should exceed the costs. Practitioners who conduct a useful evaluation project understand how it fits with other components of the program development process, and are familiar with practical evaluation procedures that can be selected and modified for the purpose. The summaries of exemplary impact evaluation studies that are included in this sourcebook indicate how specific evaluations have been related to program circumstances, how they have been conducted, and how the findings have been used. These project summaries, along with references to the professional literature relevant to continuing education program evaluation constitute a resource available to practitioners throughout the continuing education field who seek to strengthen and build support for their programs.

This sourcebook emphasizes summative evaluation to assess the impact and benefits of the program for purposes of justification and support. It gives little attention to formative evaluation for purposes of program planning and improvement. However, formative and summative evaluation are interrelated. Formative evaluation typically occurs when people associated with the program make judgments about the satisfactoriness of the program and seek to use the conclusions for program improvement. Most of the literature on continuing education program evaluation deals mainly with formative evaluation in an effort to encourage use of findings for program improvement. Because convincing evidence about program impact (such as change in performance) is difficult to obtain it is usually assumed to be associated with evidence of satisfactoriness available within the program itself (such as participant satisfaction or knowledge acquisition). While formative evaluation assumes that satisfactory process will lead to impact, summative evaluation emphasizes documentation of the extent and type of impact that results; but to improve results it must establish the connection between process and impact. Summative evaluation emphasizes application of new learnings to modify role performance, and indications of the societal benefits that result. Thus, summative evaluation to assess impact is especially important for continuing education administrators and policy makers because they are expected to justify resource allocations and resultant benefits.

It is also important to recognize that some benefits of continuing education are quite personal and are difficult to assess in such tangible ways as changed practices (parenting, food preparation) or increased economic productivity. Some continuing education programs aim mainly at such personal benefits. Examples are the Great Books discussion groups and similar study discussion programs provided by libraries, community colleges, or religious institutions. The main anticipated impact of such programs is greater appreciation of ideas and insight into issues. Assessment of this impact tends to rely mainly on self-reports by former participants regarding the personal benefits they experienced as a result of participation. It is sometimes possible to supplement this type of assessment with more tangible evidence. For example, in a community or neighborhood in which a substantial portion of adults participated in a study-discussion program, monitoring sales and library circulation of relevant books might indicate the extent to which the program influenced reading habits.

There are some concepts and procedures that summative evaluation shares with program evaluation that emphasizes formative procedures and program improvement. All program evaluation typically entails description and judgment based on analysis of quantitative and qualitative data collected from records and from various categories of people associated with the program. These categories may include adult participants, resource persons, administrators, and policy makers. Generally, in program evaluation it is desirable to focus the effort so that the benefits exceed the costs of evaluation, to obtain data from several sources to provide cross validation, and to increase commitment to the use of conclusions by involving in the evaluation process those who are to do so.

There are some concepts and procedures that are distinctive regarding summative evaluation. The emphasis on program justification to increase understanding and perhaps support by people outside the program adds to the importance of external evaluation as a guarantor of objectivity and reduced special pleading (Campbell, 1969). The reporting of conclusions to administrators and policy makers tends to emphasize brevity and written communication.

Some of the literature on assessment of the impact of programs, systems, and planned social change emphasizes taking the total system into account even when focusing on outcomes and benefits (Kirkpatrick, 1975; Katz and Kahn, 1978; Campbell, 1976). However, in many instances in which we would like proof of a program's impact, we have to settle for evidence of likely impact. It should also be noted how few follow-up studies of impact have been reported for preparatory education (Lenning, 1976).

focus on impact and benefits

One impediment to the assessment of the impact and effectiveness of continuing education is the difficulty in obtaining consensus on a few major desirable outcomes that can be readily assessed and whose results can be mainly attributed to educational activities. This problem is widespread but little appreciated in most organizations. Katz and Kahn (1978) provide some useful distinctions regarding open systems generally that can be applied to continuing education agencies.

As with most organizations, continuing education agencies have multiple outcomes that are wanted and unwanted by various constituencies. Because some goals may even be incompatible, it is usually difficult to obtain consensus on a manageable set of outcome measures. Expectations may be in conflict because of differing role perspectives and because of differing emphasis on short-term or long-term goals. For example, consider the typical views of desirable outcomes of a public university continuing medical education program from several role perspectives. A state legislator may emphasize accountability and relation to malpractice insurance. A university president may emphasize public image and coordination with other continuing professional education offerings. A professor of medicine may emphasize esoteric topics and relationships with research. A director of continuing medical education may emphasize participant satisfaction and continuation of the total continuing medical education program. A physician who participates in a program may emphasize new ideas that can be applied to practice, at a cost of time and money that seems reasonable in relation to career benefits. A patient may emphasize the health care delivered and feelings of confidence regarding the physician's performance.

From the vantage point of the continuing education administrator, assessment of impact entails more than desirability of results. It also entails organizational survival, including attention to costs as well as benefits. Costs include resources to be acquired (money, learners, teachers, facilities) as well as processes to produce results (marketing efforts, instructional activities, relations with cosponsors). Attention to the short-term impact of a continuing education agency might include little on organizational efficiency. However, long-term survival of an agency entails accumulation of some reserves in the form of money or supplies to use during hard times, and in the form of acceptance by clients and policy makers whose good will reflects the ultimate fate of most agencies. In most agencies there is a dominant coalition representing a combination of constituencies, which influences priorities and decision making. In a small, self-supporting agency, this dominant coalition may be mainly one person. In larger agencies, it does not include representatives of all major constituencies but it tends to take their interests into account. Such a coalition is seldom a formal entity but instead tends to depend on informal understandings and working relationships. The major outcomes or impacts of an agency or program, then, typically include contributions to the larger society, to the agency, and to individual participants (Katz and Kahn, 1978). Thus, multiple perspectives in the assessment of impact seem inevitable.

The short-term effectiveness of continuing education reflects both technical efficiency and power in relation to various groups. Long-term effectiveness or survival reflects accumulation of reserves, affect on contextual influences, and adaptation. For most continuing education agencies, one crucial outcome is participant acquisition of knowledge, skills, and attitudes which are applied to performance in family, occupation, and community. Most continuing education programs are alert to participant satisfaction during the program, based on the anticipation that the benefits will exceed the costs. In this sourcebook on assessing impact, the focus is on follow-up studies and other ways to evaluate the extent and types of benefits programs have for participants.

A useful approach to the assessment of program effectiveness including impact or outcomes was presented by Palola and Lehmann (1976). The approach is called Program Effectiveness and Related Costs (PERC) and is described by Lenning (1976). The relevance of PERC to continuing education is direct because Palola and Lehmann illustrate the approach with data from Empire State College. Outcomes related to student objectives include substantive knowledge, communication skills, cognitive, developmental, personal, occupational skills, public service, and unanticipated outcomes. Multiple perspectives are emphasized in data collection. Of special pertinence to assessment of impact is provision for follow-up questionnaires and interviews of graduates several years after graduation. Although the authors do not report findings regarding impact, they indicate that findings about admission to graduate school, occupational advancement, and seeking new employment opportunities could be useful for justification of college budget requests.

Some of the writings on educational evaluation generally are quite applicable to the evaluation of continuing education programs. For instance, the Occasional Paper Series of the Evaluation Center of Western Michigan University contains papers on assessing the impact of planned social change (Campbell, 1976), responsive evaluation (Stake, 1967), and meta-evaluation (Stufflebeam, 1974).

approach to impact evaluation

The most persuasive evaluation conclusions regarding impact are recent and local. In a recent volume on evaluation of continuing professional education, part was devoted to impact evaluation in fields such as medicine, public administration, social work, and library science, and very few impact evaluation studies were reported (LeBreton and others, 1979). Most of the papers indicated how important impact evaluation was, how little had been done, some of the reasons why, and how it could be done effectively in the future. The scarcity of excellent impact evaluation reports for continuing education testifies to how difficult they are to conduct. Therefore, summary conclusions from summative evaluations of similar programs can be very useful to practitioners who want to indicate the probable impact of their program. Some conclusions about impact are contained in research studies with broader purposes. Practitioners can use such findings from studies they do not conduct, both to estimate probable benefits and to select evaluation items on which to focus.

When planning any evaluation project, it is helpful to have a comprehensive framework and approach to readily consider the major parts of a potential evaluation plan and then to focus on those that are most important in a specific instance. The chapter by Grotelueschen (forthcoming) provides such a framework. Continuing education program evaluation is presented as a process that entails description and judgment which results in products or reports that contribute to decisions related to program improvement, justification, and planning. Thus, program evaluation consists of judgments, based on evidence, about program worth and effectiveness, conducted in a way to encourage those associated with the program to use conclusions for program improvement or justification. For example, *purposes* for conducting program evaluation include accounting for funds, monitoring compliance with guidelines, documenting program accomplishments, establishing program emphases, assessing collaboration opportunities, identifying content weaknesses, and assessing progress toward stated goals.

Four program *elements* that might be included in a comprehensive program evaluation are adult participants, instructors or resource persons, topics or content, and context or setting. These elements can be considered in relation to each of four program *components* —goals, designs, implementation, and outcomes. Together, these three dimensions of the program evaluation process (purposes, elements, components) provide a classification scheme to help specify evaluation questions and clarify relations among the questions.

Grotelueschen (forthcoming) lists the following eight questions that incorporate the main evaluation tasks to be accomplished:

- Purpose—why evaluate?
- Audiences—who is the evaluation for?
- Issues—what questions should the evaluation address?
- Resources—what resources are available for evaluation?
- Evidence—what evidence should be collected?
- Data Gathering—how is the evidence to be collected?
- Analysis—how can the evidence be analyzed?
- Reporting—how can evaluation findings be reported?

Such a framework can enable an evaluator to orient others associated with the evaluation process; review the total program to select the aspects on which to focus most of the evaluation effort; select available evaluation items and instruments to use for data collection; develop new evaluation items as needed; review relevant findings and procedures from comparable evaluation studies to help plan the project and interpret the findings; and relate the evaluation findings to other components of the program development process.

illustrative impact evaluations

There have been relatively few excellent examples of continuing education impact evaluation reports. Some have been for internal purposes and never published for general distribution. It is thus even more important that practitioners are familiar with exemplary evaluation reports. Some providers and settings lend themselves better than others to impact evaluation. This is especially so for agencies such as the Cooperative Extension Service of the Land Grant Universities, and the education and training departments that employers (business, industry, government, military) maintain to provide programs for their employees. Full time practitioners with support services, who have contact with the clientele before, during, and after the educational program, have much more access to impact evaluation data than do providers who depend mainly on teaching at a distance and through temporary groups and for whom follow-up studies are quite expensive.

The Cooperative Extension Service (CES) has long emphasized impact evaluation. Hundreds of studies, conducted mainly by rural sociologists on the diffusion and adoption of recommended practices, have included findings that reflect the impact of CES efforts such as bulletins and county extension advisers (Forest and Marshall, 1978; Havelock, 1969; Rogers, 1962; Rogers and Shoemaker, 1971). Ongoing local contact between CES personnel and farm families and other local residents occurs in various ways in relation to needs assessment, provision of information, encouragement of practice adoption, and evaluation. This facilitates collection of extensive follow-up data about impact over many years. It also makes it difficult to attribute to CES efforts their contribution to change, in contrast with other influences on practice adoption. A similar situation occurs for community development approaches to continuing education by any type of provider. The chapters in this sourcebook by Forest and by Boone, Fox, and Joseph report findings regarding the impact of extension programs.

Education and training departments of employers have a similar situation as they conduct educational programs for employees. The American Society for Training and Development (ASTD), the association of practitioners who conduct such programs, facilitates the exchange of concepts and practices within this segment of the field of continuing education. In addition to providing and coordinating educational programs for employees in the company, government agency, or military installation, most training directors realize that effective educational programs in such organizational settings should be closely articulated with supervision and organization development. Thus, continuing contact with employers allows access to follow-up data for the evaluation of impact on employees. Some indexes of job performance are readily used for such impact evaluations. Examples include personnel and production records regarding absenteeism and rates for production, rejects, complaints, and accidents. These indexes are usually available for employees who work in production and clerical positions. However, for some managerial and highly technical positions, clear cut measures of effective performance are less available in organizational records. The chapter in this sourcebook by Brethower indicates some of the highlights of ASTD's research conference on measuring the payoff in management training. Very few effective impact studies were reported and the conference participants mainly discussed procedures for doing so in the future. The chapter in this sourcebook by Larson reports findings from an impact study of a military literacy program that did contribute to program revision.

employers as providers

Though ASTD has emphasized impact evaluation to reflect improved performance and organizational benefits, relatively few impact evaluation reports are available. This is partly because some studies are restricted for internal use.

Kirkpatrick (1975) has compiled a book of readings organized around four foci for evaluation—reaction, learning, behavior, and results. The sections on reaction and learning deal mainly with participant satisfaction and extent of learning gain during the program, so are more relevant to internal formative evaluation than to assessment of impact. The part on behavior focuses on change of performance by participants and is very relevant to impact evaluation. It should be noted that, except for Kirkpatrick's initial set of articles, there is no discussion of results. The concluding section is on methodological problems and general advice. In the initial set of articles, Kirkpatrick notes that some results of training can be readily evaluated, such as increased production or reduced costs, accidents or grievances. However, for most continuing education programs it is difficult to separate the portion of improvements that are attributable to the educational program.

In the assessment of changed performance by individuals, Kirkpatrick urges evaluation designs that include a control group, pre-, post-, and follow-up data collection from participants and others such as supervisors, peers, and subordinates who can appraise performance. Examples of evaluation studies that emphasize change in performance are those by Stroud (1959) and by O'Rourke and Castelli (1975). Kirkpatrick discusses difficulties in assessing results but cites few published evaluation reports of such efforts. He does comment that when the educational program deals with management development or human relations training, an assessment of results is more difficult than when the program objective is as specific as reduction of accidents or absenteeism.

The following summaries of impact evaluation studies illustrate the types of studies that private businesses and government agencies have conducted to assess the results of their education and training programs for employees and others, with an emphasis on improved performance. A few studies have provided a broad assessment of results of occupationally related educational programs for adults (Berg, 1970). Most have focused on a single course or workshop.

Some impact studies have focused on orientation programs for workers who are new to a job. One example is by Gomersall and Myers (1966). An orientation was provided to reduce anxiety, accelerate acquisition of competence, and implement job enrichment. The experimental approach emphasized the very good chances for success, disregarding rumors, and taking the initiative in relating with the supervisor. A comparable control group was also used. The superiority of the experimental approach was apparent from the outset and by the end of one month

the experimental group was outperforming the control group in production and job attendance, as well as learning time. As a result, waste
and rejects were reduced to one-fifth of their previous levels, costs were
cut by one-quarter, absenteeism and tardiness dropped to one-half
of the previous normal, training time was shortened by one-half, and
training costs were reduced to one-third of their previous level.
For one hundred new hires the improvement was equivalent to savings
of $85,000.

Another use of orientation education during the first month or so
on the job is to reduce turnover, which tends to be very high and expensive in some occupations such as sewing machine operators (Lefkowitz,
1970). The approach that alternated a day of training and a day on the
factory floor for a total of three days of training produced the most satisfactory results as reflected in both low turnover and high productivity.

Another way to assess the impact of a structured continuing education program on job performance is to compare it with unstructured
on-the-job training (Cullen and others, 1976). The structured program
includes thorough job analysis as a basis for self-instructional or
instructor-based educational programs systematically designed to help a
new worker progress from zero job competence to a specified mastery.
Unstructured on-the-job training does not entail a specific program but
includes having an experienced worker provide the orientation while
continuing to perform his or her regular duties. It took less than five
hours on the average with the structured approach to achieve the criterion level of competence, compared with an average of more than sixteen hours with the unstructured approach. At the four-hour interval,
almost 90 percent competence was achieved by the structured approach,
compared with less than 30 percent competence by the unstructured
approach. The educational program costs were very similar for the two
approaches. In addition, the structured approach was superior regarding lower production losses and higher proportion of production problems that were solved.

An impact of sales training is the ability of sales representatives to
sell more products to more customers (Hahne, 1977). In one program,
the educational approach was dimensional sales training which enables
the sales representative to select a customer that he or she had been
unable to sell in the past and to develop a strategy to do so. The strategy
involves applying concepts from the seminar to all aspects of making a
sale with a specific prospect, from analyzing the prospect's needs to
closing the sale. Sales managers also participated in the educational program and provided reports on improvements in performance by the

salespersons two or three months later. Not only was the educational program considered outstandingly helpful, but more than 85 percent of the salespersons carried out their sales strategy and actually sold a previously unsellable customer.

Even when a continuing education program is conducted for employees by an employer's education and training department, which has some connection with situational influences and has substantial access to information about performance to use in assessing impact, it is very difficult to conduct a follow-up study that provides unequivocal evidence of impact.

For example, a New England company evaluated a course for first and second level supervisors to help them analyze and improve employee attendance. Data were collected from the foremen who were the course participants, follow-up attendance reviews from the managers of the participants in which they rated one trained foreman and one untrained foreman regarding analysis and correction of attendance problems, and attendance records for employees supervised by the foremen in the study.

Participants reacted favorably to the course. Pretest-posttest comparisons indicated substantial knowledge gains by foremen. A month after the course, managers rated a higher percentage of trained foremen than untrained foremen as satisfactory on every criterion. The trained foremen had more accurate records than the comparable untrained foremen, and they did more to try to improve attendance. The greatest improvement occurred when both foremen and their managers participated in the training. Actual improvements in attendance occurred more often when the manager of the foreman received training. The report also projected the dollar savings to the company if absences were reduced through such training.

One aspect of impact is implementation of training beyond the instances evaluated. In this instance, the evaluation study took eighteen months, more than a year too long to have an impact on decision making. By the time the evaluation report was available, the course was revised and then replaced.

One study evaluated the impact of a rehabilitation training program for the small minority of habitual violators who account for the majority of motor vehicle violations and accidents (Edwards and Ellis, 1976). Several thousand drivers participated in the educational program. Comparable drivers who were eligible to participate but who were not able to do so because classes were not available constituted the control group. Records of moving violations or accidents where the driver was at fault were analyzed for the year before and for the year after the educational program. The combination of being on suspension and additional driving experience contributed to some improvement of performance for drivers regardless of whether they participated in the educational program. However, for selected categories of drivers, especially young men, the educational program produced a significant improvement in performance.

continuing professional education

Impact evaluation of continuing education in each professional field has the advantage of records and contacts among members of the profession, but also has the disadvantage of the complexity of professional performance and the lack of standards and indexes of excellent performance. One field in which there has been some impact evaluation is continuing medical education. For continuing professional education in hospital settings, bi-cycle and tri-cycle approaches have used evidence of performance for both needs assessment and impact evaluation (Johnson, 1978). Although records and evaluation reports have seldom included conclusions about impact, there have been a few such cases. (Bertram and Brooks-Bertram, 1977; Manning and others, 1979; Payne and others, 1978). There is growing evidence that continuing medical education can have an impact on practice, that there are some types of learning activities that are more likely to be impactful than others, and that major impact studies can help identify specific indexes of impact that are manageable for typical evaluation use. The chapter in this sourcebook by Green and Walsh provides more detail.

One evaluation study assessed the impact of a two-day intensive continuing medical education course on the ability of practicing physicians to distinguish commonly heard abnormal heart sounds (McGuire and others, 1964). Data on gain and retention were obtained from assessment of discrimination of heart sounds during pretests, posttests, and follow-up tests six months later. Chart review was also used to assess application. All four experimental groups achieved significant gains as a result of the course, in contrast with a control group.

High initial scores were achieved by physicians who were younger, had more extensive specialized medical education regarding cardiology, had a more specialized practice regarding cardiology, and were more involved in continuing education (especially extent of reading). The amount of gain was not associated with pretest score, age, amount of previous education, nature of current practice, or continuing education participation. Participants' reactions to the course were quite positive, but variability in satisfaction did not correspond well with variability in learning gain.

Without an opportunity to practice the diagnostic procedure and to receive some reaction during the six months after the course, most participants did not retain their improved performance, and the average follow up test scores were not significantly different than the average pretest scores. Also, although chart review provided reliable and objective evidence of application of clinical know-how to patient care, it did not reveal changes attributable to the course in recording information about heart sounds. A brief report at the conclusion of the article, from an independent similar study that used a series of six two-hour weekly sessions in which posttest achievement was maintained six months later, suggests the importance of periodic instruction, assessment, and reinforcement to produce a lasting change in performance.

One of the most important studies related to the impact of continuing medical education activities on improved performance by physicians was recently completed by Payne and others (1978). The general purpose of the total study was to analyze the extent and type of impact that nonpunitive, voluntary, action-oriented, educational interventions had on the quality of physician diagnostic and therapeutic performance and improvement of ambulatory medical care delivery. Educational interventions and longitudinal data collection occurred over a period of four years at multiple sites in Michigan. The study collected data regarding performance from over a thousand physicians who specialized in internal medicine, family medicine, pediatrics, obstetrics, and gynecology.

The approach to educational intervention was based on several of the more promising previous efforts, including those reported by Payne and others (1976) and Inui and others (1976). The main aspects of the approach to produce improved performance are that (1) the physicians must perceive changed performance as useful; (2) the physician community must provide sufficient encouragement of changes to sustain initial commitment to change; and (3) there must be sufficient time for changes to be made and stabilized. Three ascending levels of intervention were included in the study. The first level was minimal, almost a control group, which consisted of reporting performance data results to the chief of clinic for dissemination to physicians providing primary care to ambulatory patients. This approximated many Professional Standards Review Organization (PSRO) quality assurance activities. The second level, in addition, consisted of several day-and-a-half workshops for the physicians themselves, which entailed reports of performance data and discussion of implications for planned change, including problem solving procedures and action planning steps. The third level added continuing consultations with hospital administrators to help them plan strategies to increase staff involvement in creating change. Some changes in management of ambulatory services also occurred.

First level intervention in the form of reporting performance data results to each site produced minimal change in performance. Second level intervention, including reporting, seminars, and corrective action planning produced significant improvement. The addition of follow-up in the third level intervention almost doubled the improvements achieved by the seminars without follow-up. Management changes further improved performance.

One of the most extensive and long standing forms of continuing education has been in-service education of elementary school teachers. As indicated in the chapter by Hentschel, very few impact evaluation studies have been conducted for such programs, but some of those that have been conducted have used changes in student achievement as a criterion of impact. For example, Helgeson (1974) analyzed the impact of about one hundred National Science Foundation Teacher Institutes by reviewing evaluation reports. Many of the reports were of follow-up studies and descriptive studies of changes in teaching performance. Relatively few studies included attention to impact on students of institute participants. In-service institutes appeared to have benefited science curriculum, teacher performance, and teacher careers. Also, the studies that included assessment of impact in the form of achievement by students of institute participants reported gain in most instances. However, it was usually not clear what portion of these gains could be attributed to their teachers' participation in an institute, in part because the gains were not always significantly different from gains by students of nonparticipants.

An impact evaluation study that demonstrated an improvement in student achievement as a result of in-service education on teaching of mathematics was reported by Koch (1973). The purpose of the in-service program was to install various teaching approaches. The evaluation report indicated that the in-service program influenced teachers to learn and use new methods and materials, as indicated by pre- and posttests at the workshop and direct observation back in classrooms. Regarding impact on students, there was an improvement on computation and understanding of concepts for all subtests, except for high ability sixth graders. There was general improvement in cognitive ability and perception of patterns, although performance in some classes was mixed. Increased creativity was substantiated by verbal measures. Based on figural measures, originality increased but attention to detail declined. There was no evidence of improvement of attitudes of students toward mathematics.

An example of an impact evaluation report prepared only for internal purposes is a follow-up study of two workshops for university administrators (Farmer and Deshler, 1974). Six months after the workshops, hour-long interviews were held with most of the participants to explore their perceptions of benefits and their reports on use of what they learned. Most administrators indicated that they had benefited from the workshops and had used what they learned. Consequences attributable to workshop experiences were quite specific, which in part reflected their focus on administrative tasks and roles such as leadership, coordination, communication, and organization development. The greatest emphasis was on feelings and perspectives regarding administrative roles, organizational relationships, communication processes, and ways to influence constructive organizational change. The respondents also reported improvements in interpersonal relations and organizational functioning, which they attributed at least in part to the workshop.

Impact evaluations have been conducted for several of the university-based Education for Public Management programs conducted under the sponsorship of the National Institute of Public Affairs during almost two decades. For example, a follow-up study of the University of Virginia program covering a dozen years between the mid-sixties and the mid-seventies was recently completed by Korn (1978). More than 80 percent of the alumni of the program for people engaged in public administration completed an anonymous questionnaire. Almost two-thirds of the participants reported that the program fostered increased interest in continuing education, more than one-third reported increased professional association activity, and more than one-third reported increased commitment to a government career as a result of the program. Personal characteristics associated with higher levels of perceived impact included applying for the program on their own initiative, expecting to increase their managerial proficiency, being under forty, and having a bachelor's degree or less.

other segments of the field

Unfortunately, in most segments of the continuing education field there are few summative evaluation reports with convincing findings regarding the impact of continuing education participation on performance in family, work, and community. There have been some, however. The following section contains summaries of impact studies that range across many areas of the broad field of continuing education. Included are adult basic education; occupational education; external degrees; libraries and counseling; continuing education of women; study discussion, self-help, and voluntary association groups. Additional impact evaluation studies on public school adult basic education and university continuing education are summarized in the chapters in this sourcebook by Fischer and Evanson, Harshman, and Giuliani.

Adult Basic Education. A national study to assess the impact of participation in adult basic education on increased literacy, earnings, and personal benefits concluded that the program did help increase proficiency in reading and math, and that for those who were working most felt that participation had helped them in their jobs and income (Kent, 1973). In a follow-up of participants in a local adult basic education program, it was concluded that participation contributed to increased employment, more reading, better use of English, and greater understanding of education. No impact was noted on participation in community groups, helping children with school work, income, or money management (Becker and others, 1976).

Sometimes the assessment of impact is against a specific criterion and is done to compare two or more delivery systems. For example, Cervero and Cunningham (1977) compared achievement on the general educational development (GED) exam between those who prepared for it by watching a television series and those who prepared for the test in some other way. The authors concluded that GED preparation by television may be a more cost-effective method of preparation for some adults, if there is some way to attract people with a good chance of passing the GED to take the test.

Career Education. The impact of occupationally related continuing education on career development has been studied as part of the National Longitudinal Surveys of the Ohio State University Center for Human Resource Research (Parnes, 1976). This survey data provided abundant evidence that adults who participated in vocational continuing education experienced greater career success than adults with similar levels of education and age who did not. For example, adults who participate in part-time or short-term work-related education typically achieve higher hourly wage rates than similar adults who do not (Adams, 1974; Flanagan, 1974; Jusenius, 1975). Also, continuing education seems to contribute to the socioeconomic level of occupational assignment (Grasso, 1975; Parnes and Nestel, 1975).

However, it is also likely that part of the apparent benefit of education reflects the selective process, in which characteristics such as levels of motivation and intelligence influence participation both in continuing education and occupational success (Adams, 1974). It also appears that vocational continuing education is more beneficial for blacks than for whites (Flanagan, 1974; Freeman, 1974).

Some studies have examined the cumulative effect of continuing education participation over the years on a general outcome such as occupational mobility. For example, Devlin (1970) compared occupational mobility patterns of participants in a community college continuing education program with similar adults who were not participants. For adults at each level of initial occupational status, participants experienced greater upward mobility than nonparticipants.

Cookson (1978) reported striking findings regarding the likely impact of continuing education participation on occupational achievement of Mexican-American small businessmen in Chicago. Path analysis was conducted on relationships among six variables. The variables were work experience (especially as a supervisor), formal educational attainment, continuing education participation, modernity of outlook, business practice adoption, and occupational achievement (mainly net earnings). Half of the businessmen in the sample were interviewed.

It appears that formal educational attainment contributes to continuing education participation and to a modern outlook. However, formal education and continuing education made equivalent contributions to a modern outlook. Continuing education participation on topics related to business apparently enables Mexican-American businessmen to acquire proficiencies that facilitate adoption of business practices associated with efficient business management, which contributes to occupational achievement in the form of net income. Formal educational attainment did not have a major influence on business practice adoption except through continuing education participation. These findings both indicate a major impact of continuing education on occupational achievement and suggest useful strategies for using continuing education to supplement work experience and to enhance formal education by increasing a modern outlook and modifying practice adoption to raise occupational achievement.

External Degrees. The University of Mid-America conducted a follow-up study of Nebraskans who had been enrolled in three television courses several years earlier. Phone interviews were completed with almost two thirds of the sample of former students. Half of the respondents continued their education in some manner, and almost half of them credited the program with a major contribution to that decision. Almost half reported that a desirable occupational change occurred since the course, and more than one third credited the program with facilitating that change. Of course, participation in an open learning course is only one format. However, it appears that more than 10 percent of the students would not have taken the courses if an open learning television format had not been available (Dolich, 1978).

One follow-up study assessed external degree graduates' experiences in employment and further study (Sosdian and Sharp, 1978). Those who complete an external degree tend to be a fairly select group of men and women with considerable prior traditional education; especially those who sought the bachelor's degree typically already had jobs so were not using the credential for initial access to the job market. Most graduates found the external degree very useful for further education and work and were well satisfied with the experience. Almost all graduates who sought access to higher-level academic programs were able to enroll. This was especially so for those who applied to mid-range institutions. A few reported problems with their external degree as a credential, especially in application to highly selective institutions. The external degree was very beneficial occupationally for most graduates, especially for women and those formerly in low prestige occupations. Most employers surveyed were very supportive of further education, including external degrees. Graduates employed in the private sector were especially likely to experience occupational benefits upon degree completion.

Libraries and Counseling. The assessment of the benefits of libraries in relation to educational activities by adults has traditionally focused on budgets and circulation. By contrast, there have been recent efforts to shift attention to the assessment of impact in the form of assistance with information seeking (Monroe, 1979). The proposed focus is on social tasks in which both society and individuals have a stake. Researchers have explored questions such as: What information was needed? Where did you turn for information? and What contribution did libraries make? There is accumulating evidence of the extent and type of impact that libraries can make on information seeking by adults (Burt, 1972; Childers and Post, 1976; Dervin and others, 1976; McClaskey, 1970; Zweizig, 1972).

One library function related to continuing education is the provision of an educational and career counseling service for adults. Two library-based Lifelong Learning Centers to serve this function were initiated in Pennsylvania in recent years, and follow-up studies of client reactions were conducted by staff of the Pennsylvania State University Center for the Study of Higher Education (Toombs and Croyle, 1977; Toombs, 1978). In each instance, specialized counseling personnel in the new learning center assembled information about educational and occupational opportunities for adults, talked with clients, and provided referrals through a network of institutions, employers, and continuing education agencies. Follow-up surveys obtained information about impact of the service in the form of outcomes reported by clients as a result of their contact with the center.

One center was established in conjunction with the Reading, Pennsylvania, public library. A variety of outcomes were reported by former clients of the center in response to the survey, including actions taken as a result of assistance provided by the center, planning and information-seeking activities, and in some instances inactivity. Half of the former clients who were sent questionnaires responded. Of those who responded, about 40 percent reported enrolling in an educational program and about 20 percent reported a major job change such as going to work or changing jobs. Thus, almost two thirds of the respondents reported that a major educational or occupational change was aided by their contact with the center. A wide variety of other outcomes were also reported including planning activities related to work and education, and a broadening of life interests.

The follow-up study report also indicates that although there is little evidence of mid-life crises leading adults to seek help from the center, many clients have feelings of dissatisfaction with their life situation. It seems likely that most of the clients were moving toward adjustments in their lives anyway, but that center services facilitated the process in many instances. The report also notes that effective interaction with counseling staff was much appreciated by clients. A parallel study of the Lifelong Learning Center of the Free Library of Philadelphia produced similar findings.

The Regents External Degree Program of the New York State Education Department conducted a follow-up study of adults who received counseling assistance from its Higher Education Library Advisory Service project. Half of those who were sent a questionnaire responded. The clients were mostly men and women seeking career change or advancement or further education, along with unemployed adults and senior citizens. Clients sought the advisory service mainly to obtain information, referral, and encouragement to pursue educational goals.

Follow-up study findings indicated that almost half the former clients had actually engaged in educational activity following their use of the advisory service, three fourths of them in higher education programs. One third said they were planning to do so, and less than one-fifth reported no follow through. Half of those who had pursued higher education activities, did so through nontraditional and continuing education programs. The report provided no indication of the proportion of former clients who were likely to have pursued educational plans and activities even without the advisory service (Dyer, 1978).

Although many impact evaluations concentrate on the adult participants in continuing education programs and what they do with what they learn, impact evaluations can also be conducted for staff development activities for continuing education teachers and administrators. Such an impact evaluation was conducted to assess the results of a three-year library staff development project in ten southeastern states to assist them in expansion of library services to disadvantaged adults (Eyster, 1976). An organization development approach was taken in which state and local library personnel in each state, along with an equal number of nonlibrarians from social agencies and adult basic education programs, helped to plan and participate in two-day workshops and ongoing support activities. The project served 936 librarians from 175 libraries at 77 sites, and even more nonlibrarians. Central to the project was local agreement on objectives to expand library services to disadvantaged adults. Also emphasized were materials and changes in practices in local libraries and communities.

The overall aim of the project was to increase the commitment and proficiency of library personnel and others so that they would achieve their objectives. Participant reactions to workshops were very positive. A follow-up evaluation of efforts at the sites indicated that major organizational changes had occurred. There was evidence of increased understanding of disadvantaged adults, development of services, cooperation with other agencies, increased community support, and changed library management. At the time of the follow up, over half of the objectives that had been undertaken were being pursued in some way. The types of objectives that the largest percentage of libraries continued to pursue were development of materials regarding coping-survival skills (more than three quarters of the libraries), in-library activities for disadvantaged adults (almost two thirds), and information and referral services (more than half). Objectives that were continued by between one third and one half of the libraries included: cooperation with adult basic education and with other agencies, outreach, books by mail, and public relations to make the library more visible to the disadvantaged. Only about one out of five libraries continued services to special groups and volunteer programs, both of which require major commitments of time and planning.

A follow-up study was conducted to assess the impact on former clients of the Career Education Project, which provided telephone counseling for home-based adults in Providence, Rhode Island, with funding from the National Institute of Education (Arbeiter and others, 1978). The project clients were mainly young women with some work experience and they were action oriented when they made contact with the project. Most of them used the counseling to find jobs or education. When they approached the project, most had occupational concerns. When they left the project, they gave more attention to further education as a next step and this was especially so for those with less education. Necessity forced many clients to take less prestigious jobs than they aspired to. A major portion of further education was obtained from community colleges, technical institutes, colleges, and universities. A majority of former clients were employed a year or two later, earning higher salaries, and were more self confident than they were before counseling. Most clients achieved what they considered a satisfactory outcome a year after leaving the project.

Continuing Education of Women. Planners of continuing education workshops sometimes follow up participants to assess impact. Rice and Goering (1977) did so for a life planning workshop, "Women in Transition." In addition to attitude change, they assessed restructuring of time and activity. Six to ten months after two workshops, a two-page questionnaire was sent to the forty-two participants, most of whom were married women in their thirties and forties who had completed one to five years of college, and 90 percent responded.

Between one third and one half of the participants reported that they felt differently about themselves or their situation as a result of the workshop. Included were increased self-esteem, self-confidence, assertiveness, and knowledgeability about their values and goals. The follow-up questionnaire contained items on time devoted to homemaking, work, volunteering, and education, both before the workshop and some months afterwards. More than three quarters reported making a change in activity following the workshop. More than half returned to school and many others made changes in work or volunteer activity. Eight people made more than one change. More than 80 percent indicated that they made decisions using information and processes learned at the workshop. Participants' ratings of the workshop at the conclusion and at the follow-up were very similar, which indicates that such ratings tend to be reliable and to persist.

Some programs that extend over several months seek to assess impact at the conclusion of the program. An example is a career development program conducted as a series of ten two-hour sessions by a university personnel office (Eng and Gottsdanker, 1979). The program included individualized self-assessment, small group career planning exercises, and total group discussion, and was attended mainly by women in clerical positions. The program evaluation obtained participants' assessment of how they might have changed during the sessions. The most widely reported changes were knowledge of how to initiate career change and improved self-image. Also included were attitude toward their own proficiency, increased communication skills, and improved attitudes toward their jobs. In an effort to assess the program's impact on career decisions, the personnel files of former participants were compared with a random sample of nonparticipants. Former participants experienced twice as many career changes, especially promotional transfers and obtaining further education. What is not clear is how much of this change reflects the orientation of those who decided to participate.

Discussion Groups and Volunteers. Davis (1961) studied the impact of adult participation in Great Books discussion groups. Members met twice a month to discuss classics of western literature. There was no evidence of change in basic values as a result of participation, but there was evidence of greater acceptance of liberal approaches to religion. Participants gained substantial understanding of local issues and problems, and there was even evidence of small increases in community activity. Participants were heavy readers when they began. Continued participation tended to increase the amount of outside serious reading. Impact was more likely to occur when participants entered the group with that outcome in mind. Deems (1979) reported that a follow-up study of participants in mid-career planning workshops showed substantial impact on career planning, work satisfaction, and job change.

A type of educational group for adults that has been expanding rapidly in recent decades is the self-help group. One of the earliest, largest, and best known is Alcoholics Anonymous. Similar groups have formed for cancer victims, check forgers, child abusers, drug addicts, ex-convicts, gamblers, juvenile delinquents, neurotics, overeaters, single parents, smokers, unsuccessful suicides, widows, and many others. Several studies have been conducted on the impact of Alcoholics Anonymous (AA) on members. Maxwell (1962) indicated the extent to which AA participation contributed to sobriety and, in many instances, personality changes such as reduction of hostility, intolerance, ego inflation, interpersonal anxieties, and an improvement of interpersonal relations. Other benefits include appreciation of life, increased sense of self-worth, greater objectivity regarding self, physical and emotional relaxation, and peace of mind. Gellman (1964) also concluded that AA has a powerful impact on alcoholics, but noted that benefits are restricted to those who are ready and able to join.

There is some overlap between participation in continuing education and participation in voluntary associations. Smith and Reddy (1973) reviewed research findings on the impact of voluntary action upon the participant, and many of the conclusions are pertinent. Facilitation of individual change is a purpose of some organizations and groups. Such organizations are most germane to continuing education. In addition, participation in volunteer activity can produce incidental learning, perhaps as a result of compliance. There are several situational characteristics that contribute to impact. One is intensiveness of influence due to moving experiences, charismatic leaders, attractiveness of position or membership, normative pressure, or dependence for satisfaction. A second is extensiveness due to multiple influences from values, examples, and group interaction and rewards. A third is consistency because various influences reinforce each other. A fourth is that the influences are enduring over time. A fifth characteristic is that the group setting contrasts markedly with prior settings and occurs when the individual is entering a new type of activity. The ability of adults to resist deliberate change efforts is reflected in findings regarding the impact of "brainwashing" and psychotherapy. The assessment of impact is difficult because individual responses to current influences are affected by experiences from the past and orientations toward the future, because multiple influences regularly occur and obscure causality, because group averages obscure individual trends, and because few effective assessment instruments are available.

benefiting from past efforts

Continuing education practitioners who seek to strengthen their use of impact evaluation can benefit from the experience of others in

24

several ways. One is in establishing organizational arrangements for evaluation that are likely to be cost-effective and to encourage cooperation and use of findings. Another is the use of procedures for sampling, data collection and analysis, and reporting likely to produce valid and convincing conclusions. A third is a broader strategy for organizational change in which impact evaluation conclusions are deliberately used for program improvement and justification. A fourth way is to draw upon the relevant professional literature for both planning an impact evaluation and interpreting the findings. Some of that literature deals explicitly with evaluation of adult and continuing education (Belasco and Trice, 1969; Byrn, 1959; Grotelueschen, Gooler, and Knox, 1976; Knox, 1969; Knox and others, 1974). Much of it, however, is from the general literature on educational evaluation which can be applied and adapted to the distinctive circumstances of continuing education (Corey, 1953; Payne, 1951; Stake, 1967; Stufflebeam, 1974; Tyler, 1969; Worthen and Sanders, 1973). A fifth way is to use meta-evaluation procedures to judge the validity and utility of the evaluation effort (Stufflebeam, 1974). Especially for practitioners who do not personally conduct evaluations, there is sometimes concern about who evaluates the evaluators and evaluation reports, and how this is done. More detailed ways in which continuing education practitioners can increase their proficiency to conduct impact evaluations are suggested in the chapters in this sourcebook by Hentschel, Rusnell, and Sjogren. The final chapter on conclusions about impact evaluation indicates clearly that continuing education can have an impact on performance and suggests program development and evaluation procedures likely to produce convincing evidence of such impact.

references

Adams, A. V. "Earnings and Employment of Middle-Aged Men: A Special Study of their Investment in Human Capital." In H. S. Parnes and others (Eds.), *The Pre-Retirement Years*. Monograph No. 15, vol. 4. Columbus: Ohio State University, Center for Human Resource Research, 1974.

Arbeiter, S., and others. *Telephone Counseling for Home-Based Adults*. New York: College Entrance Examination Board, 1978.

Becker, W. J., and others. *Adult Basic Education Follow-up Study*. Kenosha, Wis.: Gateway Technical Institute, 1976.

Belasco, J. A., and Trice, H. M. *The Assessment of Change in Training and Therapy*. New York: McGraw-Hill, 1969.

Berg, I. E. *Education and Jobs: The Great Training Robbery*. New York: Praeger, 1970.

Bertram, D. A., and Brooks-Bertram, P. A. "The Evaluation of Continuing Medical Education: A Literature Review." *Health Education Monographs,* 1977, *5* (4), 330–362.

Burt, L. N. "Bibliotherapy: Effect of Group Reading and Discussions on Attitudes of Adult Inmates in Two Correctional Institutions." Unpublished doctoral dissertation, University of Wisconsin, 1972.

Byrn, D. (Ed.). *Evaluation in Extension.* Topeka, Kans.: H. M. Ives, 1959.

Campbell, D. T. "Reforms as Experiments." American Psychologist, 1969, *24* (4), 409–429.

Campbell, D. T. *Assessing the Impact of Planned Social Change.* Occasional Paper, No. 8. Kalamazoo: Evaluation Center, College of Education, Western Michigan University, 1976.

Cervero, R., and Cunningham, P. M. "An Evaluation of the Effectiveness of Instructional Television for GED Preparation." Paper presented at the Adult Education Research Conference, Minneapolis, April 20–22, 1977.

Childers, T., and Post, J. *The Blue Collar Adult's Information Needs, Seeking Behavior, and Use.* Washington, D.C.: Office of Libraries and Learning Resources, United States Office of Education, 1976.

Cookson, P. S. "Adult Education Participation and Occupational Achievement." *Adult Education,* 1978, *29* (1), 17–38.

Corey, S. M. *Action Research to Improve School Practices.* New York: Teachers College Press, Columbia University, 1953.

Cullen, J. G., and others. "Training, What's It Worth?" *Training and Development Journal,* 1976, *30* (8), 12–20.

Davis, J. A. *Great Books and Small Groups.* New York: Free Press, 1961.

Deems, R. S. "Mid-Career Planning Workshops." In A. B. Knox (Ed.), *New Directions for Continuing Education: Programming for Adults Facing Mid-Life Change,* no. 2. San Francisco: Jossey-Bass, 1979.

Dervin, B., and others. *The Development of Strategies for Dealing with the Information Needs of Urban Residents: Phase I—Citizen Study.* Washington, D.C.: Office of Libraries and Learning Resources, United States Office of Education, 1976.

Devlin, L. E. "Participation in Adult Education and Occupational Mobility." Unpublished doctoral dissertation, University of Chicago, 1970.

Dolich, P. L. *Pre- and Post-Enrollment Behavior and Attitudes of Early Course Offering Learners in the Sun Program.* Lincoln, Nebr.: Office of Market Research, University of Mid-America, 1978.

Dyer, P. S. *Final Report on the Higher Education Library Advisory Service Project.* Albany: University of the State of New York, Regents External Degree Program, 1978.

Edwards, M. L., and Ellis, N. C. "An Evaluation of the Texas Driver Improvement Training Program." *Human Factors,* 1976, *18* (4), 327–334.

Eng, J. E., and Gottsdanker, J. S. "Positive Changes from a Career Development Program." *Training and Development Journal,* 1979, *33* (1), 3–7.

Eyster, G. W. *Final Report: Expanding Public Library Services to Disadvantaged Adults.* Morehead, Ky.: Appalachian Adult Education Center, Morehead State University, 1976.

Farmer, J. A., Jr., and Deshler, J. D. *Evaluation Report: A Leadership Development Program for Academic Department Chairmen, and Consultation Skills for University Personnel.* Los Angeles: Graduate School of Education, University of California, 1974.

Flanagan, R. J. "Labor Force Experience, Job Turnover, and Racial Wage Differentials." *Review of Economics and Statistics,* 1974, *56* (4), 521–529.

Forest, L. B., and Marshall, M. B. *Impact of Extension in Shawano County.* Madison: University of Wisconsin-Extension, 1978.

Freeman, R. "Occupational Training in Proprietary Schools and Technical Institutes." *Review of Economics and Statistics,* 1974, *56* (3), 310–318.

Gellman, I. *The Sober Alcoholic: An Organizational Analysis of Alcoholics Anonymous.* New Haven, Conn.: College and University Press, 1964.

Gomersall, E. R., and Myers, M. S. "Breakthrough in On-the-Job Training." *Harvard Business Review,* 1966, *44* (4), 62–72.

Grasso, J. T. *The Contributions of Vocational Education, Training, and Work Experience to the Early Career Achievements of Young Men.* Columbus: Center for Human Resource Research, Ohio State University, 1975.

Grotelueschen, A. D. "Evaluation." In A. B. Knox (Ed.), *Adult Education Program Development and Administration.* San Francisco: Jossey-Bass, forthcoming.

Grotelueschen, A. D., Gooler, D. D., and Knox, A. B. *Evaluation in Adult Basic Education: How and Why.* Danville, Ill.: Interstate, 1976.

Hahne, C. E. "How to Measure Results of Sales Training." *Training and Development Journal,* 1977, *31* (11), 3–7.

Havelock, R. G. *Planning for Innovation.* Ann Arbor: Center for Research on the Utilization of Scientific Knowledge, Institute of Social Research, University of Michigan, 1969.

Helgeson, S. L. "Impact of the National Science Foundation Teacher Institute Program." Research Paper No. 16, Minnesota Research and Evaluation Project, Minneapolis: College of Education, University of Minnesota, 1974.

Inui, T., and others. "Improved Outcomes in Hypertension after Physician Tutorials." *Annals of Internal Medicine,* 1976, *84,* 646–651.

Johnson, C. F. "Bicycles, Tricycles, and Continuing Medical Education." *Journal of the Tennessee Medical Association,* May, 1978, 345–351.

Jusenius, C. L. "The Influence of Work Experience and Typicality of Occupational Assignment on Women's Earnings." In H. S. Parnes and others, *Dual Careers.* Monograph No. 21, vol. 4. Columbus: Center for Human Resource Research, Ohio State University, 1975.

Katz, R., and Kahn, R. "The Concept of Organizational Effectiveness." In R. Katz and R. Kahn (Eds.), *Social Psychology of Organizations.* (rev. ed.). New York: Wiley, 1978.

Kent, W. P. *A Longitudinal Evaluation of the Adult Basic Education Program.* Falls Church, Va.: System Development Corp., 1973.

Kirkpatrick, D. L. (Ed.). *Evaluating Training Programs.* Madison, Wis.: American Society of Training and Development, 1975.

Knox, A. B. "Continuous Program Evaluation." In N. Shaw (Ed.), *Administration of Continuing Education.* Washington, D.C.: National Association for Public School Adult Education, 1969.

Knox, A. B., and others. *An Evaluation Guide for Adult Basic Education Programs.* Washington, D.C.: U.S. Government Printing Office, 1974.

Koch, R. R. *Mathematics Inquiry in the Conrad Area, 1972–73 Outcome Evaluation Report.* Wilmington, Del.: Conrad Area School District, 1973.

Korn, A. R. "The Education for Public Management Program at the University of Virginia." Unpublished master's thesis, University of Virginia, 1978.

LeBreton, P. P., and others (Eds.). *The Evaluation of Continuing Education for Professionals: A Systems View.* Seattle: Continuing Education Division of Academic and Professional Programs, University of Washington, 1979.

Lefkowitz, J. "Effect of Training on the Productivity and Tenure of Sewing Machine Operators." *Journal of Applied Psychology,* 1970, *54* (1), 81–86.

Lenning, O. T. (Ed.). *New Directions for Higher Education: Improving Educational Outcomes,* no. 16. San Francisco: Jossey-Bass, 1976.

Manning, P. K., and others. "Continuing Medical Education: Linking the Community Hospital and the Medical School." *Journal of Medical Education,* June 1979.

Maxwell, M. "Alcoholics Anonymous: An Interpretation." In D. J. Pittman and C. R. Snyder (Eds.), *Society, Culture, and Drinking Patterns.* New York: Wiley, 1962.

McClaskey, H. C. "Bibliotherapy with Emotionally Disturbed Patients: An Experimental Study." Unpublished doctoral dissertation, University of Washington, 1970.

McGuire, C., and others. "Auscultatory Skill: Gain and Retention after Intensive Instruction." *Journal of Medical Education,* 1964, *39* (2), 120–131.

Monroe, M. E. "Social Task Orientation of Library Use: A First Step Toward Measuring Impact of Public Library Service." Unpublished proposal. Madison, Wis.: University of Wisconsin, School of Library Science, 1979.

O'Rourke, P., and Castelli, J. A. "A Follow-Up Study on Supervisor Training." In D. L. Kirkpatrick (Ed.), *Evaluating Training Programs.* Madison, Wis.: American Society for Training and Development, 1975.

Palola, E. G., and Lehmann, T. "Improving Student Outcomes and Institutional Decision Making with PERC." In O. T. Lenning (Ed.), *New Directions for Higher Education: Improving Educational Outcomes,* no. 16. San Francisco: Jossey-Bass, 1976.

Parnes, H. S. "Current Issues in the Relationship Between Manpower Research and Policy." Special Report No. 7. Washington, D.C.: National Commission for Manpower Policy, 1976.

Parnes, H. S., and Nestel, G. "Factors in Career Orientation and Occupational Status." In H. S. Parnes and others, *Dual Careers.* Monograph No. 21, vol. 4. Columbus: Ohio State University, Center for Human Resource Research, 1975.

Payne, B. C., and others. *The Quality of Medical Care: Evaluation and Improvement.* Chicago: Hospital Research and Educational Trust, 1976.

Payne, B. C., and others. *Method of Evaluating and Improving Ambulatory Medical Care.* Ann Arbor: University of Michigan, College of Medicine, Department of Post Graduate Medicine, Office for Health Services Research, 1978.

Payne, S. *The Art of Asking Questions.* Princeton, N.J.: Princeton University Press, 1951.

Rice, J. K., and Goering, M. L. "Women in Transition: A Life-Planning Workshop Model." *Journal of the National Association for Women Deans, Administrators, and Counselors,* 1977, *40* (2), 57–61.

Rogers, E. M. *Diffusion of Innovations.* New York: Free Press, 1962.

Rogers, E. M., and Shoemaker, F. F. *Communication of Innovations.* New York: Free Press, 1971.

Smith, D. H., and Reddy, R. D. "The Impact of Voluntary Action Upon the Volunteer/Participant." In Smith, D. H. (Ed.), *Voluntary Action Research: 1973.* Lexington, Mass.: Heath, 1973.

Sosdian, C. P., and Sharp, L. M. *The External Degree as a Credential: Graduates' Experiences In Employment and Further Study.* Washington, D.C.: National Institute of Education, 1978.

Stake, R. E. "The Countenance of Educational Evaluation." *Teachers College Record,* 1967, *68,* 523–540.

Stroud, P. V. "Evaluating a Human Relations Training Program." *Personnel,* 1959, *36* (6), 52–60.

Stufflebeam, D. L. *Meta-Evaluation*. Kalamazoo: Western Michigan University, Evaluation Center, 1974.

Toombs, W. *A Study of Client Reactions. Lifelong Learning Center, The Free Library of Philadelphia*. University Park: Pennsylvania State University, Center for the Study of Higher Education, 1978.

Toombs, W., and Croyle, G. E. *A Client Reaction Analysis: Final Report for the Lifelong Learning Center, Reading, Pa.* University Park: Pennsylvania State University, Center for the Study of Higher Education, 1977.

Tyler, R. W. (Ed.). *Educational Evaluation: New Roles, New Means*. Chicago: University of Chicago Press, 1969.

Worthen, B. R., and Sanders, J. R. *Educational Evaluation: Theory and Practice*. Belmont, Calif.: Wadsworth, 1973.

Zweizig, D. L. "Predicting Amount of Library Use: An Empirical Study of the Role of the Public Library in the Life of the Adult Public." Unpublished doctoral dissertation, Syracuse University, 1972.

Alan B. Knox is professor of continuing education at the University of Illinois at Urbana-Champaign, where he serves as director of the Office for the Study of Continuing Professional Education. This office has been active in the development of instruments and materials and in conducting workshops to help continuing education practitioners become more proficient in program evaluation.

Higher test scores for basic skills or passing the GED test are insufficient evidence of Adult Basic Education program impact. To discover if programs are really affecting learners' life situations, follow-up studies and anecdotal data provide more pertinent information.

test scores don't tell the whole story

joan keller fischer
jane l. evanson

The ultimate goal of Adult Basic Education (ABE) is to improve students' life situations. Since the inception of the federally funded ABE Program, emphasis has been on general development of basic skills to bring students to an arbitrary grade level equivalent and to prepare them to pass the General Educational Development (GED) examination. Individual program success is typically measured by the number of people who pass the GED test or by the degree to which students increase their achievement test scores. Additional program data that are reported to the federal government include such information as numbers of people who no longer receive welfare, who registered to vote, or who obtained drivers licenses. Although this type of information relates to program success, it does not adequately describe the full impact of ABE instruction nor does it indicate the extent to which people have improved their life situations.

To adequately ascertain if the goal of ABE has been met for

people entering at all levels, more conscientious and systematic attempts must be made to evaluate all facets of programs. Four such attempts will be reviewed in this chapter, each emphasizing a different aspect of ABE programs. These attempts provide data regarding the impact of programs on people's lives and also suggestions for other evaluators.

evaluating the effects of certification

An evaluation study to find out if completion of high school programs had fostered participation in additional education or training, or improved employment situations was conducted in Iowa (McClurg, 1977). Because there were difficulties obtaining data from local programs, only those completers whose records were on file with the state office were included in the study. Two mailings, sent to 3,900 people who had completed the high school program one to two years previously, yielded a 36.8 percent response.

When asked why they had enrolled in programs, the former students cited personal satisfaction (52.9 percent), pursuit of further education or training (21.9 percent), employment (14 percent), job promotion (2.2 percent), or military enlistment (3.4 percent). Responses regarding current status, however, indicated that 34.3 percent had enrolled in educational or training programs, the majority of which were vocationally related. Those not employed had dropped from 33.7 percent to 20.5 percent with 22.4 percent reporting that they had begun employment. Another 8.3 percent reported receiving job promotions, while 4.1 percent were in the military. In contrast to the 5.3 percent who indicated that they were attending school prior to ABE enrollment, 15.1 percent were in school at the time of the survey. Of the 563 who changed jobs, 29.8 percent attributed that change to obtaining the certificate.

It appeared that a secondary school certificate provided a vehicle for upward mobility. Moreover, considering the stated reasons for entering the programs and the reported changes in status, it appeared that possession of the certificate created new options. Responses from employers who were surveyed as part of the evaluation indicated that they regarded the secondary certificate favorably for both employment and promotion, even if the certification was not required for initial employment. It seemed, then, that the certification rather than the means of obtaining that certification was the vehicle. To the extent— which was not evident from the report—that programs increased skills which led to certification, those programs could be considered successful.

evaluating program data

In Pennsylvania the intent of a recent statewide evaluation was to collect data that would assist in improving program administration and effectiveness (Lindsay and others, 1976). The evaluators adapted Mezirow's perspective discrepancy evaluation model and surveyed 272 staff and 1,580 students from 60 programs in regard to 6 program component areas. Survey data, which were presented in a follow-up workshop to staff members, provided a basis for developing recommendations to improve program operations. This procedure was more appropriate to evaluating program process than impact on students' lives. Some data, however, did relate to student satisfaction.

The data that were available indicated that students enrolled to get a high school equivalency diploma (35 percent), to improve self (33 percent), and for employment reasons (19 percent). Almost all the students (97 percent) felt that the classes were helping them reach their goals. When asked about their learning gains in reading, writing, and math and increased reading outside class, approximately 65–75 percent reported that attending ABE classes had helped "very much" or "some."

evaluating broader program impact

To assess the broad impact of ABE participation in Ohio, Boggs and others (1979) surveyed former students three years after they had left the program. The survey questions sought to find out if students' occupational status had improved, if students' had been further assimilated into society, and if personal goals had been met. Students' responses were compared to those of a control group of ABE eligible but nonparticipating adults.

From an estimated potential former student population of 9,654 people, 351 from 12 programs were interviewed by phone. The control group consisted of 1,500 people. Stratified random sampling procedures were employed to select participants in both groups. A comparison of ABE students surveyed, the total population of 1973–74 ABE students, and the control group indicated that the two ABE groups were somewhat similar in sex, race, and residence characteristics. The control group, however, was quite different from both ABE groups, and consisted of far more white and older people.

Overall, former ABE students were *relatively* more positive in their responses than those in the control group. Several significant differences for items related to social involvement, employment, child-school relations, voting, home ownership, and education were found for the responses of the two groups. Since participating in ABE, former students said they were more likely to read magazines, use social services, be secure in jobs, be registered to vote, and so on. In contrast, nonparticipants said they were more likely to continue friendships, communicate easily with school personnel, and own homes. Some of these differences could have been a function of the differences in the characteristics of the two sample groups.

Several interesting findings were observed when further analyses of the relationships of ABE sample characteristics and responses to specific impact indicators were completed. For example, nonwhites tended to report negative impact while whites tended to report positive impact. Income was not dramatically affected for any group. A surprising finding was that levels of reading and math ability, the degree of improvement in these skills, and the extent of participation time were often correlated negatively with impact behaviors. The evaluators stated that, "Prolonged attendance and maximum achievement may not be necessarily linked to positive benefits in other life areas" (Boggs and others, 1979, p. 128).

It was also observed that well over half the students answered "yes" when asked if they had enrolled to increase reading and math skills and to pass the GED. Students were not questioned about reasons for enrolling other than those related to basic skills. While almost all former students said they had improved basic skills abilities, only 40 percent reported passing the GED. Perhaps those who most wanted and were most capable of passing the GED focused their efforts on this goal. Other students may have had other, less precise goals, or realized after entering that they did not want to devote the time and energy necessary to passing the GED. They may have been more likely to relate new learning to other activities in their lives.

It must be noted that the data were based on students' perceptions and that no information was available regarding actual extent of activities at any point in time for either group. Nevertheless, the responses did suggest that ABE participants benefited in ways other than increasing basic skills or passing the GED. The evaluators attributed the positive effects to the total ABE experience, but noted that impact could be increased. They suggested a greater emphasis on content that would be directly related to adult functioning and competencies to improve this impact.

evaluating life skills instruction

Several years ago, a cooperative project involving the Adult Education Resource Center at Worcester State College and six New England adult learning centers was initiated to promote life skills instruction for ABE students. The evaluation of the project sought to find out if this instruction succeeded in increasing students' knowledge of life skills and their ability to deal with life situations.

Both formal and informal procedures were used to gather information for the evaluation. At the beginning and end of instruction, the Adult Performance Level (APL) Survey was administered to students enrolled in the classes. Test data were supplemented with student questionnaires and student and teacher interviews. In addition to these procedures, regular and frequent project staff meetings provided information relative to the project objectives. Findings indicated that participants learned about the topics studied.

Questionnaire and interview data further indicated that teacher and student reactions to the instruction were positive. The interview data indicated that students thought they had improved in such areas as meeting people, keeping healthy, improving English, learning about community, learning about money, learning about government, learning about jobs.

Although the test and interview data were positive, program personnel did not think that the full impact of the instruction was evident. The instruments used provided little specific information as to whether the students were actually *using* knowledge and skills that had been gained through instruction. Even the questionnaire responses were too general and dealt more with life skills knowledge and perceived gains. Anecdotal data, derived from conversations and visitations with staffs and students, provided more cogent evidence that instruction had actually affected participants' lives. This type of data was not systematically collected; however, specific incidents of individual applications of skills were frequently reported by staff members at regularly scheduled meetings. Because such stories related so directly to the project goals, an effort was made to collect as many as possible throughout the project.

An example was the story of Paul, a disabled, sixty-year-old carpenter who had just lost his wife. When he entered a life skills class, Paul was lonely and felt inadequate because he lacked basic skills. An injury from his last job made it impossible for Paul to do hard physical work, and the adult education class provided a daily activity. Paul began to experience success when for the first time he completed his own savings deposit and withdrawal slips as a result of instruction in banking. He was proud that he no longer had to ask the teller for assistance. Later, he opened his first checking account; ultimately, with knowledge about and trust in banking services, Paul purchased a six month Certificate of Deposit. During the time he was involved in life skills instruction, Paul mended both psychologically and physically as laughter, friends, and real economic gains changed his life.

Connie was a spunky sixteen-year-old from Portugal. She had two serious problems—a cleft palate and an inability to communicate well in English. In spite of her problems, she handled translations and business transactions for her entire family. Connie participated wholeheartedly in life skills English as a Second Language classes; solving the problem of her cleft palate became a concern of everyone in the center. Through instruction, the entire class learned about the community resources (for example, Red Cross, clinics, therapy) related to Connie's problem, the use and completion of medical forms and applications, the importance of emotional support through difficult times, and the role of interpersonal relations in problem solving. Within a year, Connie's life had changed almost completely; her new self-image emerged along with her fluency in English, the elimination of her physical problem, and her faith in other human beings.

Before entering adult education, Betty's world had fallen apart. At age forty-five, her husband had left her with the responsibility for four children and two totally disabled parents. Her education was minimal due to early responsibility for younger brothers and sisters. These experiences left Betty with an extremely low self-image and a feeling of hopelessness about her future. Life skills instruction in the area of occupational knowledge motivated Betty to look for and find a job that was appropriate for her. Later, instruction in consumer economics resulted in the purchase of a car for which she set up her own financial arrangements. With a great sense of accomplishment from improving her life, she managed to save enough money to enjoy a vacation with her children. Emotionally, academically, and financially Betty clearly benefited from life skills instruction.

These were only three of the instances where it was evident that students were using the learning acquired through life skills instruction. Yet, though they represent the very essence of what programs are striving to do, such valuable data never appear on traditional program reports. Nor are such specific incidents likely to be immediately recalled by students years after they have left the program.

It would be helpful to develop a simple form to document instructional effects as staff members become aware of learning applications among students. A possible format for life skills instruction is suggested in Figure 1. The list of benefits was culled from the types of applications observed in New England life skills classes. Specific applications of skills can be listed in the second column. For example, next to "attempted an activity independently for the first time" the instructor could write "completed savings deposit and withdrawal forms." A separate sheet could be kept for each student to document individual benefits. To gather the information, staff members could hold periodic meetings with individuals or with groups of students. This procedure would not only help them acquire the information for the program, but it would demonstrate to students how they are benefiting from participation and might provide motivation for further applications of skills.

Figure 1. A Possible Format for Life Skills Instruction.

Skills Student Demonstrated or Reported:	*Specific Applications of Skills:*
1. Attempted an activity independently for the first time	
2. Changed a behavior in dealing with own life situation	
3. Resolved a personal or immediate problem	
4. Took steps toward dealing with a life situation	
5. Helped other people with newly learned skills	
6. Completed own form outside of class	
7. Acquired information that helped in making a decision	
8. Acquired information that aided in asking questions	
9. Made a major decision related to class activities	
10. Gained access to a resource related to a personal problem	
11. Used a process learned in the program to identify and use resources on own	
12. Showed greater awareness of agencies from which help can be gained and increased tendency to use resources	
13. Expressed greater confidence in dealing with specific life situations	

conclusion

The evaluation studies reviewed in this chapter suggested that students respond positively to many different aspects of ABE instruction, that instruction increases basic skills and helps people to pass the GED test, that certification increases options for further steps, and that instruction affects students' life situations in specific ways. The studies also suggested models for evaluating program practices and impact. It was clear, though, that further documentation and appropriate recording devices for that documentation are necessary to fully comprehend the impact of instruction.

references

Boggs, D. L., and others. "Adult Basic Education in Ohio: A Program Impact Evaluation." *Adult Education,* 1979, *29* (2), 123–140.

Lindsay, C. A., and others. *1975–76 Pennsylvania Adult Basic Education Assessment Project: An Examination of the APL Construct and Mezirow's Program Evaluation Model as a Basis for Program Development.* University Park: Adult Basic Education Section, Department of Education, Pennsylvania State University, 1976.

McClurg, R. B. *Assessing the Effect of Adult High School Completion Programs on Graduate Placement.* Aukeny, Iowa: Des Moines Area Community College, 1977.

Joan Keller Fischer is associate director of Community Affairs and associate professor of adult education at Worcester State College in Massachusetts. She has been a teacher, teacher trainer, researcher, and administrator of adult education. She is noted for her research on the GED examination and competency-based education.

Jane L. Evanson is a dedicated adult educator who was director of the Adult Education Resource Center when the New England life skills project began. She has extensive background as a professor of adult education, teacher trainer, and writer of materials for ABE/GED programs. Most recently, she has served as chairperson of the ABE Commission for the Adult Education Association.

Assessment of impact is generally regarded as a desirable
and important activity, but there are several important
issues to consider before undertaking an impact assessment.

the Shawano County
impact evaluation

laverne b. forest

What impact does University of Wisconsin-Extension have in a single
county? How many citizens are reached by Extension over a year or a
decade? What impression do these contacts have on participants? What
benefits do people perceive as a result of the contacts? These questions,
along with an interest in learning better methods to evaluate impact of
extension education efforts, prompted the Shawano Impact Evaluation
project.

university of wisconsin-extension

The University of Wisconsin-Extension system may seem very
complex and overly organized. However, given its philosophy and purposes, it is actually quite simple. President VanHise stated in 1905, "I
shall never be content until the beneficent influence of the University
reaches every home in the state" (Vance, 1960). This philosophy, known
as "The Wisconsin Idea," entails providing knowledge from all disciplines, to all residents regardless of their distance or location from Uni-

versity campuses. Much of this knowledge is disseminated in relation to problems or needs of citizens.

Herein lies the perceived complexity: To attempt to reach all citizens requires many program emphases. Wisconsin has thirteen. The emphases provide educational programs around the following themes: Agriculture and Agribusiness, Business and Industry, Communications, Engineering-Mathematics-Applied Sciences, Education, Government and Community Development, Family Living, Health, Human Resource Development, Natural and Environmental Resources, Social Services, School for Workers (Labor), and Youth Development. Furthermore, given the variations in content and potential audiences, varying staffing patterns and methods are used to reach people. Some Extension staff members operate statewide, some at district levels, and some within counties; also, depending on content and audience, various combinations of educational techniques such as two-way telephone conferences, meetings, printed materials, demonstrations, expositions, citizens' advisory committees, consultations, and mass media are used.

the impact evaluation process

The above brief description of University of Wisconsin-Extension illustrates that an apparently simple question like "How many people do we reach?" is really not so simple. This dilemma thus became the basis for developing the more systematic approach to assessment of impact reported here (Forest and Marshall, 1978). In this system, eleven major tasks were identified and completed:

Selection of the County. Given the pilot nature and the intensiveness of this evaluation, only one of the seventy-two Wisconsin counties was selected to be evaluated. Shawano County was selected because it is representative of other rural counties in Wisconsin and the North Central region of the United States. In addition, the potential clientele was diverse.

Developing Support for Evaluation. To increase the probability that results would be accepted and used, much time was given during the early project stages to inform all Extension administrators and statewide program leaders, Shawano County Extension staff, and Shawano County citizens and leaders. This process increased their understanding, their cooperation, and the quality of the evaluation itself.

Staffing and Resources. This pilot evaluation's purposes were to evaluate more areas than one study normally would, so as to learn more about what should be evaluated in the future and what should not be. Thus, the county staff did not carry the entire burden of the evaluation tasks of data gathering, interpretation, and communication of results. In addition to the project codirectors, a half-time research assistant was hired for the duration of the project; two ad hoc people from Shawano County did local data gathering; and telephone interviewing was subcontracted to a professional survey office.

Program Inventories. Because the expected evaluation was to assess impact and consequences of all Extension efforts in the one county, a complete listing of already conducted programs was necessary. The ad hoc staff working with project codirectors developed comprehensive descriptions of all Extension programs and activities in the county from 1960 to 1975. These summaries not only were part of the evaluation, but also defined the limits of the program to be considered in surveys.

Thus, the Shawano evaluation considered all aspects of Extension's impact in the county as one. The following efforts were part of the summaries and were evaluated:
- Both Shawano agent and statewide specialist activities in the county;
- Activities in and outside the county in which residents participated;
- All of Wisconsin's 13 program areas;
- All methods including mass media, group, and individual contacts;
- Extension efforts with various groups and communities;
- Repetitive contacts over a multiple-year period (15 years).

Many sources of data were used to document Shawano County programs. Office records, annual reports, project files, circular letters, agent vitae, news files, Wisconsin Extension Management Information System (EMIS) data, and records on noncredit program offerings from state-based departments and specialists were all used to develop Extension program summaries.

The program summaries were used by special task forces in deciding survey content and focus. The summaries also documented the extent of certain long-range efforts as they occurred over several years—a story that was not as apparent when looking at single-year efforts. The additive effects of continuing sequential programming became much more evident through this activity.

Based on our experiences, we recommend that evaluators: (1) Prepare a comprehensive summary(ies) for the program time period to be evaluated; (2) Save professional time, if possible, by hiring ad hoc people who are somewhat familiar with Extension; (3) Review not only county records, but those of other Extension units; (4) Use documentation for planning data collection and evaluation; (5) Share documentation with potential users of evaluation data.

Task Forces. Small groups of administrators, program leaders, specialists, district directors, and Shawano agents reviewed the program inventories. Along with advisory committees, these task forces made suggestions about the type of evaluative data they would find useful and how data ought to be gathered. This activity was intended to increase the likelihood that the information would eventually be used.

Data Collection. Once potential users of impact data had identified the data they felt would be important, it was decided that through telephone survey interviews perceptual data would be gathered because: (1) It is easier to collect than scientific observations of actual behavior; (2) Voluntary Extension programs depend as much on perceived value as on actual value; (3) It entails less cost in money than experimental observation or personal interviews; (4) Testimonies and feelings of people are easily understood; (5) Participants could mentally review all of their experiences and arrive at additive effects and benefits due to several contacts.

Two groups were interviewed in early 1976: Leaders, and the General Public. In the Leader Survey, 238 people (or about 85 percent of those identified) were interviewed who held an elected or appointed office or were considered leaders by people knowledgeable about county and community affairs. The General Public Survey consisted of interviews with a random sample of 1,192 residents, eighteen years or older. Answers to an early question separated those who had considerable contact with Extension from those who had little or none. The former group was then asked many more questions than the latter.

The questions in the survey obtained data related to levels 3–7 of the Bennett hierarchy. These include: (3) Participation, (4) Reactions, (5) Learning Change, (6) Practice Change, and (7) End Results (Bennett, 1976, p. 4).

For level 3 (Participation), answers to the following types of questions were used to describe the extent and type of contact with Extension.

18. Now I have some questions about the number of times you have attended various types of Extension meetings in the past fifteen years. After I read a description, would you indicate whether—over the years—you have attended such meetings ... never, less than fifteen times, fifteen to thirty times, or more

than thirty times . . . meetings where a Shawano Extension agent presented information?

23. Have you been in individual contact with a Shawano Extension agent through any of the following means: A. visit to your home, farm, or business? B. by telephone or letter.

For level 4 (Reactions), questions of the following nature were asked of those who participated in Extension programs in any way.

31a. In general, how helpful is the information in bulletins to you . . . a lot, some, a little, or no help?

104. In general, how would you rate Extension . . . as excellent, good, fair, or poor on each of these things? (A) . . . being worth the tax money invested? (B) . . . being effective in helping people? (C) . . . being efficient in carrying out its work?

For level 5 (Learning change), participants were asked these types of questions:

31e. What was the topic of the *one* Extension bulletin you best recall reading?

26. Please give me examples of two or three things you learned at the meeting.

For level 6 (Practice Change), participants were asked the following types of questions about whether they used or applied any ideas (Rogers, 1962).

31f. Did you use anything from this bulletin—and if so— how did you use it?

12. Please think for a second about some specific information which you have gotten. Then give me an example of what that information was, how you used it, and what that meant to you or to others.

Finally, level 7 (End Results) was determined by asking participants to what extent they themselves and the county had benefited from Extension as follows.

83c. How much difference did the program seem to make in what your children ate . . . a lot, some, or no difference?
(Leader Survey)

11. Extension has worked with various groups to various extents. From your knowledge of Extension, how much have the following groups benefited from its programs in Shawano County? Would it be a great deal, some, little, or none? How much have (a) elderly? (b) parents & homemakers? (c) professionals & businessmen? (d) farmers? (e) Indians?

Respondents were asked whether they or their communities had benefited in any of six ways. Based on major value systems and representative of long-term goals for human endeavors, six types of benefits (Forest, 1973) were used to categorize responses showing how Extension efforts in various and diverse ways contributed toward central themes in people's lives. Among these benefit types are: economic improvement; government improvement; home, health, and safety improvement; development of individuals' abilities; improvement and preservation of the natural environment; and expansion of educational resources.

Preliminary Data Summaries. Tabulations of various responses and percentages from survey data were prepared for immediate sharing with members of task forces, advisory committees, and other interested Extension staff. This effort stimulated potential users' interest in the data by asking for their judgments and interpretations.

Standard Setting. Evaluation has not occurred without comparison of *what is* (data) with an expression of *what should be* (standard, criterion, desired level of performance). Standards can be established by relying on (1) a similar situation, (2) "experts," (3) research, and (4) personal beliefs.

In this evaluation, standards were set by asking 60 Extension individuals and 10 county leaders 100 questions such as, "What percentage of the adults in Shawano County should have had contact with Extension in any way during the past fifteen years?", and "What percentage of families should have had a child in 4-H at some time?" They did this in group meetings and through the mail *prior* to looking at the data. The procedure alerted them to soon-to-be revealed data and helped them get personally involved in the data.

Extension personnel's standards varied greatly as to what percentage of people should have Extension contact. For instance, the desired percent of contact with Extension ranged from 18 percent to 100 percent, with the mean being 62 percent.

In summary, all future impact evaluations should set standards at or near the time of data collection and reporting. Specific procedures can vary, but the general process is a must for several reasons:

- Data are meaningless without personal reference points.
- Multiyear Extension programs involving adults evolve from original goals, and thus original goals, if they existed at all, are not very useful as a reference point.
- Users of data are not likely to be the same people who set the original five- to fifteen-year-old goals and thus do not automatically accept them.
- Cross-discipline or multiple-unit program evaluations are less likely to have standards to which data can be compared.
- Setting criteria motivates potential data users to actually use the data.
- A criterion that a data user sets becomes a commitment.
- The setting of criteria is a learning process for data users.

To reiterate, evaluation is not just measurement, or proving impact, or determining the attainment of educational objectives. Instead, program evaluation is determining the worth of Extension's total efforts by comparing actual contacts, reactions, and so on (measurements) with what is desired (criteria) (Steele, 1970, 1975).

Thus, this project gave much time and used several approaches to exploring implications and reaching conclusions. Project team members identified themes in data, major conclusions, and possible implications for accountability or programming, shared them at meetings, and by mail, and at meetings focused discussion on the meaning of the findings.

In sum, many people helped disseminate and interpret results. The following conclusions can be made: (1) Interpretation, analyses, and reaching implications are time consuming and difficult; (2) Data have little value unless users help to develop conclusions and interpretations; (3) Individuals and groups need stimulation through presentations and discussions to come up with implications; (4) Because of diverse values, needs, interests, philosophies, and criteria of Extension staff, interpretations are also diverse. As such, each interpretation is valid in itself; (5) More time must be given to learning about developing interpretations and implications of evaluations.

Communication of Results. The Shawano evaluation shared findings in many ways: (1) long narratives; (2) short summaries; (3) short brochures highlighting findings on a particular topic and announcing the availability of longer papers; (4) audiovisual media such as transparencies; (5) group meetings with Shawano County agents and leaders

and other district, state, and national Extension staff; (6) the series of
three major reports, including the book *Impact of Extension in Shawano:
1. Conclusions and Implications;* and (7) many one to one contacts. Bar
graphs were used to support narrative reports, depict data, and show
further analyses (Forest and Marshall, 1977).

Based on our Communication of Results experiences we found
that potential users of evaluation findings must be personally involved.
A personal involvement is more easily secured through pleasant, informal sharing where data are easily understood. Consider the time available to audiences and their commitment to being involved. Reinforce
points with words and visuals. Do not ask people to wade through sixty-
four pages first, then send them a one-page highlight three weeks later.
Arrange the reporting of evidence according to how people learn:
awareness, involvement, acceptance, practice, and change.

We also learned that two-by-two slides are less conducive to group
sharing and discussion. Invest in overhead transparencies that help or-
ganize information according to major findings and conclusions, but are
very flexible.

Evaluating the Evaluation. As a pilot effort, the nature and extent
of usage of the evaluation results by Extension staff primarily in Wisconsin were measured to see what should be done in future similar evaluations. These data, along with additional recommendations for what data
are useful, comprise *Impact of Extension in Shawano County: 3. Usage and
Appraisal* (Forest and Marshall, 1979). Thus, Extension people who had
participated in the evaluation (referred to as the core group) and random samples of other Extension people in Wisconsin and professionals
in other states were asked to fill out a questionnaire in the fall of 1978.
This questionnaire asked them how they used the results, if at all, and
what questions they would recommend for future similar evaluations.

Overall, 39 percent of all people (52 percent of the core group), in
response to an open-ended question, gave general supportive statements
for the evaluation; 22 percent said it was very timely, useful, and relevant; 12 percent said it had limited usefulness; and 11 percent said it
would become a guide or model for others to follow.

Because evaluations should be useful, respondents were asked if
they used or benefited from the evaluation results in various ways. Table
1 presents responses relative to benefits.

The responses in Table 1 show several things. First, the core group
consistently perceives more benefit while the non-Wisconsin group
(those most psychologically distant from the evaluation) perceived less

benefit. Second, the higher levels of benefits (improved decision making and accountability) received less responses than the lower levels of benefits. Third, when considering all responses, this follow-up found a great deal more usage than the project directors anticipated or hoped for. These findings were encouraging because a great deal of literature and comments by practitioners are along the theme that formal evaluations are not used, therefore, why do them? Reconsider if this is your belief; your evaluation results *will* be useful if evaluations address specific concerns.

All program evaluation situations are unique and the evaluator will have to collect data to answer key questions pertaining to that situation. However, the positive responses we received clearly demonstrate the relative usefulness of data types in an impact evaluation (Forest and Marshall, 1979). It would be worthwhile to take these responses into account when designing evaluations.

Table 1. Perceived Benefits from Evaluation Results

Level of Benefit or Usage[a]	Statement	Group	Percentage Responding yes
Decision Making	"I made decisions about next year's programs based on results."	Core Wisconsin Non-Wis.	23% 12 5
Accountability	"The evaluation showed that Extension has done what it said it was doing."	Core Wisconsin Non-Wis.	26 20 6
Learning	"I've learned about Extension methods in Shawano."	Core Wisconsin Non-Wis.	39 35 30
Motivation	"I've been stimulated to a new way of thinking about programs and their value."	Core Wisconsin Non-Wis.	29 9 7
Communication	"I've distributed some of the results to others."	Core Wisconsin Non-Wis.	61 9 28

[a]The hierarchy of benefits from evaluation has been substantiated by both a panel of 25 "evaluation experts" prior to this study and by the three groups of respondents in this evaluation. (Forest and Marshall, 1979)

Table 2. Shawano Evaluation Results and Data Found Useful

Type of Data Found Most Useful	Group	Percentage Yes Responses
1. Percent of Contact/Participation through various methods like radio, meetings, TV	Core Wisconsin Non-Wis.	65% 53 30
2. Percent of contact/participation by specific group, such as farmers, villagers, low income	Core Wisconsin Non-Wis.	58 33 28
3. Percent of overall Extension contact	Core Wisconsin Non-Wis.	55 38 28
4. Perceptions of types and amounts of benefits from Extension	Core Wisconsin Non-Wis.	52 29 37
5. Reactions and judgments about Extension efforts	Core Wisconsin Non-Wis.	52 24 33
6. Conclusions and implications based on data	Core Wisconsin Non-Wis.	45 24 28
7. Data related to specific programs or projects	Core Wisconsin Non-Wis.	39 19 21
8. Data on leaders contacts and perceptions	Core Wisconsin Non-Wis.	39 15 30
9. Types of information received from Extension	Core Wisconsin Non-Wis.	36 24 21
10. Perceived priorities and needs of people	Core Wisconsin Non-Wis.	32 18 14
11. Data on standards and criteria for judging results	Core Wisconsin Non-Wis.	32 8 23
12. Ideas used or practiced by people	Core Wisconsin Non-Wis.	23 14 16

(Forest and Marshall, 1979)

summary

This evaluation was very costly, time consuming, and complex to insure that we would learn more about the evaluation process. Much was learned about what impact evaluations should be like in the future. The general overall recommendation reached was that program impact evaluations be planned and carried out according to the constraints, concerns, available resources, time, skills, and other practical considerations of the given program situation. This brief chapter gives but a few hints on how to do that.

references

Bennett, C. F., *Analyzing Impacts of Extension Programs*. Washington, D.C.: United States Department of Agriculture, Federal Extension Service, 1976.

Forest, L. B., "Using Values to Identify Program Needs." *Journal of Extension*, 1973, *11* (3), 24–34.

Forest, L. B., and Marshall, M. *Impact of Extension in Shawano County, 1. Conclusions and Implications*. Madison: University of Wisconsin-Extension, 1977.

Forest, L. B., and Marshall, M. *Impact of Extension in Shawano County, Methodology*. Madison: University of Wisconsin-Extension, 1978.

Forest, L. B., and Marshall, M. *Impact of Extension in Shawano County, 3. Usage and Appraisal*. Madison: University of Wisconsin-Extension, 1979.

Rogers, E. *Diffusion of Innovations*. New York: Free Press, 1962.

Steele, S. "Program Evaluations, A Broader Definition." *Journal of Extension*, 1970, *7* (2), 5–17.

Steele, S. "An Emerging Concept of Program Evaluation." *Journal of Extension*, 1975, *13*, 13–22.

Vance, M. M. *Charles R. VanHise: Scientist Progressive*. Madison: Wisconsin Historical Society, 1960.

Laverne Forest was a county agricultural agent in Minnesota for eight years prior to assuming his current role as evaluation specialist in Program and Staff Development, University of Wisconsin-Extension. He is an associate professor in Continuing and Vocational Education on the Madison campus.

Two impact studies indicate advantages for the assessment
of benefits of extension programs.

continuing education evaluation: looking back, looking forward, thinking through

edgar j. boone
robert d. fox
harold j. joseph

The need to assess the impact of adult and continuing education programs is one of the most important challenges confronting continuing educators. Never before has more emphasis been placed on accountability for program and outcomes—to the program users as well as to those who allocate funds for continuing education programs. The overriding question today is whether or not continuing education programs are making a difference in the quality of living of those persons who are taking advantage of program offerings.

Programming in continuing education includes three interrelated processes—planning, implementation, and evaluation. Although evaluation has always been viewed as an integral process of programming, it has received the least emphasis. This lack of emphasis can be attributed to a number of factors. Program evaluation, to say the least, requires mastery of evaluation concepts and skills. A survey of in-service education and graduate programs designed for training continuing educators reveals that little attention has been given to teaching them how to evaluate programs.

The decision to apply human and material resources to a given problem is always made at the expense of other problems. Pressures arising from this inherent dilemma and the sense of personal and professional responsibility among decision makers often are manifest in attempts to evaluate continuing education programs.

Several applied research studies have been conducted in North Carolina to assess changes in adult learners and subsequent changes in their performance. This chapter reviews two evaluative studies describing the assessment of continuing education efforts in terms of: the educational outcomes that were expected as a result of participation in the programs, the method employed for evaluating the subsequent outputs and outcomes, the results of the evaluation, and how the results were or could be used by practitioners in terms of improving policy decisions or educational processes, or as justifications for new or continuing allocations of human and material resources to future programs.

evaluation of printed media effectiveness

The North Carolina Cooperative Extension Service has as one of its purposes the improvement of nutritional practices of people. A study by Trent and others (1976) measured the effectiveness of three types of printed media—cartoon booklets, information leaflets, and circular letters—in disseminating basic food and nutrition information to low-income homemakers in North Carolina. It also examined the relationships between knowledge and practice change and personal and situational characteristics of the participants. It was assumed that if the media examined in this study were an effective means of reaching low-income families on a mass basis with food and nutrition information, perhaps the same approaches might be used in communicating information on a variety of topics, such as improved farm practices, economic concepts, public policy concepts, and land-use planning.

The objective of this continuing education program was to provide low-income homemakers with knowledge of good nutrition or dietary practices. This evaluative study was designed to describe two dimensions—outputs and outcomes—of the impact of these media on change in existing nutrition practices. The output dimension was the extent to which participants' knowledge of desirable nutritional practices increased according to the type of media used to disseminate knowledge. The outcome dimension was the extent to which the nutritional practices of participants changed after receiving different media.

A random sample of 864 homemakers was selected from a total population of 11,050 homemakers who had participated in the Expanded Food and Nutrition Education Program (EFNEP). These homemakers were divided into four groups—three experimental and one control. The experimental groups received nutrition information through leaflets, circular letters, or cartoon booklets over a six-week period. All groups were interviewed before and after the period in which the materials were distributed.

Analysis revealed a significant change in both nutrition knowledge and practices among all homemakers in the study. The greatest knowledge change occurred in the experimental group that received the leaflet, while the greatest change in practices occurred in the group that received the circular letter. However, the degree of knowledge change and practice change did not differ significantly according to the type of printed media received. Likewise, no significant relationship was found between knowledge and practice change and characteristics of the participants.

The information gained from this study could be useful to decision makers in two ways. First, it substantiated the utility of certain printed media as means for increasing nutrition knowledge and changing nutritional practices of low-income homemakers. Second, it reinforced the utility of applying resources to the dissemination of information through printed media.

evaluation of decision-making and communication patterns

In a second study (White and Boone, 1976), the characteristics of 130 of North Carolina's disadvantaged farm families (DFF) were analyzed to ascertain the types of farm and home decisions made by these families, the rationality of their decision-making process, the sources of information used by the families in making decisions, and the linkage between sources of information cited by the respondents and research-based sources.

The findings revealed that DFF engage in a wide range of decisions that require knowledge and expertise in several different areas and that the DFF exhibit rationality in their decision making. The sources of information most cited and used for decision making were interpersonal—family, neighbors, and friends. These interpersonal sources were not closely linked to a research base, which indicated inadequate communications or communications barriers between continuing educators and DFF.

The major reason for such communications barriers may be the relationship between the change agents and the DFF. The difference between the change agent and the DFF in personal and social characteristics may direct the DFF to seek information from individuals with whom they have more in common than change agents. Unfortunately, such homogeneous interpersonal relationships seldom bring about an exchange of scientifically based information. Thus, there is an implied need for more training of individuals from the disadvantaged segment to serve as intermediate sources in transferring to DFF pertinent information from research-based sources. This approach would be similar to utilizing the interpersonal communications that appeared to be so important to the DFF.

conclusion

These examples are representative of the applied research projects in continuing education that have been completed or are underway in North Carolina, and indeed, the whole United States. As a relatively new and growing field, continuing education is making strides in discovering and developing relevant concepts and precise methods for assessing the effectiveness of its programs in terms of content, outputs, and outcomes. The two studies reviewed here reflect a strategy of evaluation in which the outputs of participation in continuing education programs were emphasized equally with the outcomes. Moreover, each of the studies was based on concepts that have application beyond the scope of merely describing what is "good" and what is "bad" about a particular program. Each of the studies was designed to generate response useful for the planning and management of individual learning experiences, and to provide continuing educators with additional understanding of social and educational processes. Broadly based evaluations of this type not only contribute to refining programs. They also contribute to the body of knowledge that may be applied to the total field of continuing education. They are the tools that help us look back, look forward, and think through!

references

Trent, C., and others. *The Effectiveness of Cartoon Booklets, Information Leaflets, and Circular Letters in Disseminating Basic Foods and Nutrition Information to Low-Income Families.* Center for Rural Resource Development Report No. 3. Raleigh: North Carolina Agricultural Experiment Station and North Carolina Agricultural Extension Service, 1976.
White, E. E., and Boone, E. J. *Decision Making and Communication Patterns of Disadvantaged Farm Families in the North Carolina Coastal Plains Area.* Tech. Bull. No. 245. Raleigh: North Carolina Agricultural Experiment Station, 1976.

Dr. Edgar J. Boone, past-president of AEA/USA, is head of the Department of Adult and Community College Education and assistant director, North Carolina Agricultural Extension Service, North Carolina State University, Raleigh.

Robert D. Fox is a research intern with the Southern Association of Colleges and Schools and a doctoral candidate in Adult and Community College Education at North Carolina State University.

Harold J. Joseph is an instructor of English at Peace College, Raleigh, North Carolina, and a doctoral candidate in Adult and Community College Education at North Carolina State University.

As part of a comprehensive quality assessment effort one study surveyed the impacts of a nontraditional degree upon graduates of the program.

the impact of the nontraditional degree: a case study

carl l. harshman

In 1973, Saint Louis University, a comprehensive Jesuit, urban institution, initiated nontraditional associate and bachelor's degree programs for adult learners. The programs were located in Metropolitan College which, to that point, served as the University's noncredit continuing education center. The University initiated degree programs in the areas of business studies, liberal studies, and urban affairs. In 1974, the College joined the School of Nursing and Allied Health Professions in offering a Bachelor of Science in Nursing exclusively for persons with a Registered Nurse diploma or an associate degree in nursing.

The College operates as an autonomous undergraduate unit. Degree requirements, academic policy, courses, and the like are developed through the College. There are no full-time faculty; the University's faculty and practicing professionals are contracted to teach on a course-by-course basis. The College has a schedule of three twelve-week terms with a six-week summer session. About 40 percent of the classes are held on the main campus; the rest are offered at off-campus centers in the metropolitan area. In addition to course work, credit is granted through examination, by evaluation of noncollegiate sponsored instruction, and through portfolio evaluation of experiential learning.

About 85 to 90 percent of the students are employed full-time. There are larger proportions (compared with other undergraduate programs in the University) of women and black students and most students indicate career goals as the rationale for pursuing a degree.

developing a model for assessing quality

During the early years of operation, there were concerns about the quality of the program. As a result, Metropolitan College began exploring the issue of quality in higher education. Based on the literature on higher education, the concept of quality appeared vague and traditional definitions of quality tended to be process oriented (such as curriculum content, student-faculty ratios, credits earned) rather than product oriented (such as what students had learned). Further, there seemed to be a tendency to apply the same quality standards to programs designed to serve a diversity of populations and educational needs.

A proposal to study the concept of quality in nontraditional programs was written to and eventually funded by the Ford Foundation (Harshman, 1979). The goals of the project were:

1. To explore and develop the concept of quality in educational programs in order to achieve a better understanding of it.

2. To analyze evaluation methodologies as they might apply to nontraditional programs in higher education.

3. To design a quality assessment model that meets certain stated criteria for the evaluation of nontraditional programs.

4. To test the model on a nontraditional program.

The project was carried out through a steering committee composed of professionals from various areas of higher education such as accreditation, state-level coordination, and outcomes assessment.

The remainder of this chapter sketches the model and contains a synopsis of the assessment of impacts on students—a survey of Metropolitan College graduates from 1974 to 1976.

the quality assessment model

The model resulted from an analysis of elements of a nontraditional program in terms of open systems concepts. The result is a view of a program in terms of its *environment, inputs, structure and functioning,* and *outputs.* Each element is defined through a taxonomy that contains components, subcomponents, and sources of evidence (data) for each. Evaluation methodology provides the means to make operational the information entry, coding, and response mechanism of an open system. In the model, the activities of evaluation are categorized according to: (1) Foundations Phase (deciding on the basis for the evaluation—for example, program goals); (2) Information Phase (identifying sources of evidence, collecting and analyzing data); and the (3) Judgments Phase (drawing conclusions, analyzing cause and effect, and making program-related recommendations). The model brings the three kinds of activities of evaluation to bear on each element of the program.

The model is adapted to specific programs through the use of a locally selected steering committee which, in conjunction with persons responsible for the program, (1) identifies the appropriate foundations for the evaluation and sets priorities among them, (2) selects the appropriate sources of evidence and decides how data will be collected and analyzed, and (3) decides how judgments will be made and who will make them.

the impact study

Four studies were conducted as a pilot test of the model. One focused on an employer's perceptions of the College and its programs; a second focused on the quality of the College's student services; the third involved an analysis of the College's finances; the fourth study was concerned with assessing some outcomes for students. With increasing attention being given to the effects on and benefits to students, the impact study was considered essential. A project carried out by the Bureau of Social Service Research (Sosdian and Sharp, 1978) under a contract from the National Institute of Education (NIE) was helpful in making a conceptual model for the study.

Quality Questions. The following questions were the basis for the survey of Metropolitan College graduates:

1. How important were various goals for the graduates and to what extent were the goals attained as a result of the education?
2. In what ways did the students benefit from the degree?
3. To what extent do the graduates perceive personal gains from the degree?

4. How do graduates compare an education at Metropolitan College to that of other nontraditional programs? To established programs?
5. To what extent did the experience affect career or employment?
6. What was the expected effect of the degree on the graduate's job? What actually happened?
7. What were outcomes in terms of new employment or postbaccalaureate education?
8. How do the graduates rate their overall satisfaction with Metropolitan College?

Methodology. The population for the study consisted of the graduates of Metropolitan College from 1974–1976 (N-188). A local instrument was developed from one used at Metropolitan State in Minnesota (Sosdian and Sharp, 1978) and one created for a survey of Saint Louis University graduates (Career Planning, 1978). The instrument was mailed in the spring of 1978.

Results and Conclusions. Of the 188 instruments distributed, eighty-six (47 percent) were returned and useable. Seventy-two percent of the respondents were men. The majority of respondents had earned a business degree (57 percent); 24.4 percent were urban affairs graduates; 17.4 percent had received a liberal studies degree. (Because the nursing degree is awarded through the school of Nursing and Allied Health Professions, the alumni are not considered to be the College's and, hence, did not participate in the study.)

The data were analyzed and respective item options reported as percentages of the total. The independent contractor that conducted the study reviewed the results and offered his conclusions. Subsequently, the project review committee served as the judgment team for the pilot studies, reviewed the results, and critiqued the researcher's conclusions. The committee members were: Robert Kirkwood (Middle States Association), Oscar Lenning (NCHEMS), Richard Peterson (ETS), Rev. Paul C. Reinert, S. J. (Saint Louis University), Janet Ruyle (CRDHE, University of California, Berkeley), John Shea (Carnegie Commission on Policy Studies in Higher Education), and Carl Trendler (Bureau of Higher Education-Rhode Island).

The conclusions agreed upon by the researcher and the project review committee were:

1. Career related goals and the satisfaction of having a degree were or are most important goals for a number of the graduates; enjoyment of learning is not a high priority goal.

2. The benefits of a degree tend to parallel the goals priorities. In addition, however, about one-fourth of the alumni indicated that the degree as a "stepping-stone" to further education is the most important benefit.

3. Most of the goals are instrumental rather than intellectual. The personal gains data support what might have been inferred from previous data.

4. When rated against other nontraditional programs, the alumni perceived Metropolitan College to be somewhat better. They are, however, less positive when comparing the College to more established programs.

5. The degree appears to correlate with increased entry into middle-management positions and with a major increase of entry into professional and top-level management.

6. Expected and actual changes related to the job were consistent. Increased pay, responsibility, and respect from coworkers were indicated as expected by over 60 percent of respondents. In each case the "happened" percentage was high.

7. In general, it appears that graduates do not seek (or do not find) work with new employers, but rather that advancement and other rewards occur with the current employer.

8. Of the graduates who applied for admission to graduate or professional school (47 percent), 83 percent were admitted. Of those admitted who enrolled, about 15 percent saw their undergraduate experience as limiting them in their graduate work.

9. Over 90 percent of the graduates were satisfied with the degree and with the quality of the educational program.

The most important impacts reflected above are (1) the career (instrumental) orientation of these graduates, (2) the extent of occupational improvement after receiving the degree, and (3) the pride these graduates take in their education.

using the results in the college

The ultimate purpose of the model is the infusion of results into the College. Because the College is still in the midst of completing the project, work with the results of the pilot study has only begun. Regardless, it is possible to look at some of the results of the impact study and identify implications for the future of the College. Some of the possibilities are described below.

Upward Career Mobility with Same Employer. An implication of the fact that graduates seem to move up within the same organization rather than move to new fields or employers pertains to such services as the University Office of Career Planning and Placement (CPPC). If most graduates (wish to) remain with current employers, then the traditional emphasis of placement is not essential to the graduates. As an alternative, CPPC could provide more career development programming for the mature student. This office currently offers a range of nonplacement services used primarily by younger undergraduates including off-campus work experience internships and a four-module career development course for credit.

Perceptions of the Quality of the College. As the results indicate, the sample of graduates perceived this nontraditional program as better than others of which they were aware, but not quite as good as more traditional programs. The results are judged to be valid especially because of the College versus traditional program data. The question, however, is: Should the College be concerned about upgrading its quality or about changing its students' perceptions?

adapting the approach to other programs

The increased need for impact data will probably move other programs to evaluate their impact on their graduates. The value of a general evaluation is that it helps the approach be more comprehensive, such as by including data about environment, students entering the program, program structure and functioning, as well as outcomes. At the same time, however, it is possible to design and conduct an impact study such as the one reported without simultaneously conducting related studies. The major limitation is that it may be difficult, if not impossible, to interpret results and to ascertain the causes of certain phenomena.

If an impact study is needed, the following suggestions are offered: (1) Compare the goals of a program to the range of possible outcomes for students (see Harshman, 1979; Lenning, and others, 1977) to decide which outcomes are appropriate to and important for the program.

(2) Identify appropriate sources of evidence (data). Standardized instruments, locally constructed instruments, interview data, or unobtrusive data should be considered. There is a value placed on bringing multiple sources of evidence to bear on a particular question (Kunkel and Tucker, 1977).

(3) Using a qualified researcher-evaluator in instrument construction, data collection and analysis, and descriptive report writing has several benefits. For one, the probability of error through methodology is reduced. Second, the conduct of the study is not dependent upon the limited time of program personnel. Third, the judgments are negotiated among, for example, the evaluator, program personnel, and judgments team members.

These suggestions along with concerns such as an explicit and public commitment to make use of the data should result in valid information for decisions about the quality of a program.

references

Career Planning and Placement Center. "Arts College Alumni Survey." *Universitas* (Saint Louis University), 1978, *3* (3), 8.

Harshman, C. L. *A Model for Assessing the Quality of Non-Traditional Programs in Higher Education.* St. Louis, Mo.: Metropolitan College of Saint Louis University, 1979.

Kunkel, R., and Tucker, S. "A Perception-Based Model of Program Evaluation: A Values Oriented Theory." Paper presented at annual meeting of the American Educational Research Association, New York, April 1977.

Lenning, O., and others. *A Structure for the Outcomes of Postsecondary Education.* Boulder, Colo.: National Center for Higher Education Management Systems, 1977.

Sosdian, C., and Sharp, L. *The External Degree as Credential: Notes on Methodology.* Washington, D.C.: Bureau of Social Science Research, 1978.

Carl L Harshman is the dean of Metropolitan College of Saint Louis University and an associate professor of Higher Education. As a result of his experience with this nontraditional program, he authored the proposal for and directed the project on the assessment of quality.

Impact evaluations of two continuing higher education programs illustrate the use of criteria for selection of programs likely to warrant the investment in an assessment by such studies.

selecting continuing higher education programs for impact evaluation

betty giuliani

If not all continuing education instructional programs can or should be evaluated for impact, how does the program administrator decide which activities to follow up for effect? One criterion might be the extent to which the duration and intensity of a program could realistically be expected to produce measurable change in participants or in their organizations. Another might be the availability of program support for the evaluation process itself (with support defined as time, money, evaluation expertise, and faculty cooperation).

The two programs reviewed in this chapter meet these two tests. The first, the Michigan Governmental Accounting Program, resulted from the passage of legislation that mandated change in local governmental unit accounting procedures. The length of the program and the support available were sufficient to warrant an impact study. The nature of the changes to be made demanded that impact evaluation be done.

The second, the Institute for Criminal Justice Executives held at the University of Chicago, was funded by a government grant that required an impact evaluation. The design of the program and the resources available at the University were especially appropriate for such a study.

In both programs, the evaluation design included measurements of cognitive gain and participant satisfaction that were used to shape the course of the educational experience in progress. The major emphasis in each case, however, was the determination of impact on participant behavior and organizational process.

the michigan governmental accounting program

With the passage of a state law requiring all local units of government to use the Michigan Uniform Accounting System, the Michigan State University Institute for Community Development (ICD) began a cooperative program planning venture with the state Treasury Department and the Statewide Association of Local Governments. A series of programs was developed to educate government officials in the implementation and use of the Uniform Accounting System (UAS).

The first program in the series was a fifty-hour course in basic fund accounting, offered at numerous locations around the state and necessitated by the fact that most local treasurers, clerks, and other government officials had little or no education or experience in this area. The second program in the series was a workshop, held on the University campus, which assisted local officials with the conversion of their "old" systems to the Uniform Accounting System. The third program in the series was introduced three years after the first two were initiated. It was a conference for Certified Public Accountants (CPAs), who are required by law to perform the audits on local governmental account books.

Each program in the series required the development of special texts and supplementary materials. Instructors were selected for demonstrated competence in the field and were given an orientation to ensure their ability to handle both the technical and the political aspects of the program. The involvement of the Treasury and the local governments association assured that both local and state officials would be represented in all aspects of development, delivery, evaluation, and response.

The evaluation of individual participant learning was measured in the traditional manner; that is, the fifty-hour course provided opportunities for measurement of cognitive gain through written tests, recitations, and practical assignments. The conversion workshops were designed to produce a set of books to be taken back to the local government unit and used. Following these two parts of the program, instructors from the courses and the workshop visited a sample of local government units that had participated in the program and spent from a half to a full day working with the government officials on any problems which might have arisen in implementing the system. Finally, the annual audit by independent CPAs provided the Treasury Department, the Institute for Community Development, and the government association with specific evidence of successful and unsuccessful adoption of the uniform system.

In the eight years since the program was started, all but about 10 percent of the local government units in Michigan are using the uniform system. About 15 percent of those units using the system have had major problems identified by the auditors. This is clear evidence of the success of the educational programs in changing individual participant knowledge and behavior, as well as in affecting the operations and practices of local governmental units. At the state level, both the Department of the Treasury and the legislative Fiscal Agencies have been affected by the changes occurring at the local level. For the first time, there is a common data base available that permits analysis and evaluation of the uses of state and federal revenues expended locally. This, in turn, shapes legislative planning.

As to the educational program itself, it is still in operation—modified to meet new or changing needs of local officials and CPAs as the uniform system is further refined and improved. Additional services have been provided to the Treasury Department by ICD in the form of a reaction reporting procedure from the local units to the State (Wolenberg, and others, 1979).

the institute for criminal justice executives

The Institute for Criminal Justice Executives was supported by a grant from the Law Enforcement Assistance Administration/National Institute of Corrections (LEAA/NIC) to the University of Chicago Center for Continuing Education. The Chicago Institute was the first of seven similar institutes held at various locations around the country between 1972 and 1977.

Participants attending the Chicago Institute were selected by NIC; of the forty-three in attendance, thirty-one volunteered, five had been assigned to come, and the remainder had both "volunteered" and been invited. Members of the group came from twenty-six states, worked in federal, state, county, or municipal agencies, and represented juvenile and adult corrections, law enforcement, and adult and juvenile community treatment programs. The only major area within the criminal justice system which was not represented was the judicial.

The Institute design consisted of three phases. Phase 1 was a three-week workshop, held at the Chicago Center, that included three major substantive areas: a management component covering leadership, problem solving, and management by objectives; an evaluation component; and, a criminal justice component. Resource experts in each substantive area were responsible for the development and presentation of relevant materials and information. Phase 2 covered a nine-month period during which participants returned to their jobs and could, if they wished, carry out work projects developed, in part, during Phase 1. In Phase 3, participants returned to the University for a one-week workshop during which, in addition to covering new material, a selected sample of work projects was reviewed.

A team of program evaluation consultants designed and applied evaluation instruments and procedures throughout the three phases of the Institute. The evaluation effort had two main foci: The first was to ascertain the extent to which meaningful changes in the participants' learning had occurred as a result of their exposure to the Institute; the second was the "systems impact evaluation," which sought to ascertain whether any of the learning acquired during Phase 1 had been transferred back to the organizations from which the participants had come.

In order to collect information bearing on participant change, the evaluation team conducted interviews with participants and faculty, administered a variety of questionnaires and opinion surveys, held informal discussions, and collected participants' work project diaries. A 25 percent sample of participants was interviewed on the job during Phase 2 of the program.

The systems impact evaluation relied on a questionnaire survey of the participants six months after the close of Phase 1 and an identical questionnaire survey of a sample of the participants' staff members. This technique provided two separate sources of information on the behavior changes of Institute participants "back home" and an inference about the changes in the organization.

Analysis of the data collected on individual participant learning and change indicated that the level of management skill practiced by many of the participants was raised as a result of the Institute experience. The Institute also provided a stimulus to participants for undertaking and accomplishing Phase 2 work projects. Finally, there was evidence to support the belief that the participants who did change their behavior when they returned to their organizations had a positive effect on their colleagues and subordinates. The NIC achieved greater visibility and recognition as a result of the Institute, another hoped-for outcome of the program. A number of outcomes suggested ways of improving the planning and execution of such institutes for criminal justice executives in the future (Nowlen, 1973).

summary

Although impact evaluation studies are not easy to design and conduct, the two examples reviewed in this chapter demonstrate that, when certain conditions exist, the task can be made less difficult to carry out and may be given some guarantee of success. One such condition appears to be *a multipart, time-spaced program design.* Both studies are of this design and the impact evaluations took advantage of that fact.

The multipart, time-spaced design allows for growth and change to occur in the participants and in their organizations, serves to strengthen the participants' commitment to the program objectives (if the program has relevance), and provides positive reinforcement to those individuals who put new practices into operation. This makes it a desirable educational format. And the evaluation design is also enhanced; first, because the time lapses between program parts can be utilized to measure changes in participant behavior and the effects of changes on the organizations from which the participants come. In addition, the measurement of effects resulting from the first part of a program can be conducted during the succeeding parts of the program.

A second condition present in both exemplary programs, appears to be that the program content, whatever the subject matter, stress *application of skills and knowledge.* This allows program planners to specify behavioral objectives in operational terms and provides an opportunity for desired behaviors to be exhibited and measured within the organizational setting.

references

Nowlen, P. M. *Institute for Criminal Justice Executives: Final Report.* Chicago: University of Chicago, Center for Continuing Education, 1973.

Wolenberg, J., and others. *Michigan Comparative Local Unit of Government Fiscal Report* (Report to Michigan Department of Treasury). East Lansing: Michigan State University, Institute for Community Development, 1979.

Betty Giuliani directs the Office of Operations Research and Analytical Studies, Continuing Education Service, Michigan State University. She has also been active in research and evaluation projects of the National University Extension Association.

Not knowledge gain but changed performance on the job
was the central issue of this evaluation conference.

ASTD conference on evaluating the payoff of management training

karen searles brethower

In the fall of 1978 the American Society for Training and Development (ASTD) sponsored the First Annual Invitational Research Seminar on evaluation. It was organized to encourage impact evaluation. This chapter summarizes some of the presentations and indicates key points from the discussion. Highlights of the conference are contained in the recent article by McNamara and Salinger (1979). The proceedings will be published by ASTD later this year (Peterson, 1979).

Evaluation has long been viewed as important to training and development in organizations. In part, this importance is due to competition for funds. As profits are squeezed, the pressure to assess the impact of training increases. One of the effects of long term attention to evaluation has been to differentiate between various types of evaluation. The Kirkpatrick (1976) steps of evaluation and the Brethower and Rummler (1976) levels of evaluation are commonly used models. Kirkpatrick identifies four steps: (1) reaction, (2) learning, (3) behavior, and (4) results.

Results include reduced costs and improved efficiency. Brethower and Rummler (1976) present four similar levels in an evaluation matrix that also addresses: what might be measured, measurement dimensions, sources of data, data gathering methods, and evaluation criteria for each. Both articles cover the fundamental choices facing an evaluator in a field environment. Kirkpatrick (1976) also summarizes some of the key evaluation studies in business related training and development.

Following are brief summaries of two of the impact studies reported at the conference. Each indicates something of the evaluation approach and findings.

A government department in a midwestern state undertook a demonstration project to improve management effectiveness in local agencies. The project included two types of continuing education with an emphasis on improved managerial performance to improve organizational climate and thus agency performance as perceived by staff members. One continuing education approach consisted of management development with an emphasis on management education, technical assistance, and self-help tools for managers. The organization development approach combined management education and organization developments for all members of the agency, which included a Worker Initiative Process Workshop. The results of the management development approach were mixed, with slight positive or negative shifts in climate and perceived agency performance, but no clear trend. The organization development approach was very successful in improving agency climate. However, agency performance was only slightly improved. For both approaches, the complexity of influences on agency performance and limitations of the study design restricted explanations of reasons for results. The recommendations were about continuing education program development and evaluation generally and were not one approach or the other. Improvement in climate and performance occurred in a local agency in which there was no intervention. The main influence was attention by state level management to local management problems. This indicates the importance of assessing unintended influences and consequences as well as achievement of objectives.

Most evaluation reports are for internal use and not for distribution outside the company. Following is an example drawn from an evaluation report on a management development program of a national food processing company. The program deals with topics such as problem solving, delegation, and time management. Before the program, participants are provided an overview of each session and are asked to state their personal goals and expectations for the session. During the program they assess the on-the-job helpfulness of each session. At the end of the program they prepare personal action plans to be implemented within six months. One copy of these plans is sealed in an envelope and returned six months later with a follow-up evaluation request for a report on change in performance as a result of the program. The resulting evaluation summary contains both numerical ratings and written comments.

The evaluation conclusions indicate that most first level supervisors apply what they learn and produce results that warrant company investment in the management development program. The written comments were grouped according to stage of adoption of new concepts and practices, in categories such as the following: I understand my job better, and it's improved my performance; I've added to the responsibilities of my job; I've blended what I've learned with how I used to do things; I've added new skills to how I do my job; I've used this information in specific situations.

Regarding program impact on supervisor performance, the following comments are indicative of participant applications of concepts related to major topics of the program. (1) Management—"has helped pull our sales team together to enjoy a record year." (2) Communications—"have learned to be a better listener and obtain reactions from employees so I know they understand." (3) Problem Solving —"applied the four steps when I had to place a sales representative on probation, and today he is one of my better employees due to the way the situation was handled." (4) Organization—"provided a good understanding of line and staff, and cleared doubts about which was which." (5) Leadership—"became more versatile with various approaches, depending on the people and the problem to be solved." (6) Motivation—"helped me turn a poor performer into a top performer." (7) Writing—"my written communication is now short, simple, and understandable." (8) Accident Prevention—"our accident rate has decreased, the first aid type injuries are fewer. I can more easily find the cause of the accident and correct it, rather than the cause of the injury." (9) Meetings—"my meetings have shown definite improvement." (10) Complaints—"helped me to handle complaints constructively rather than destructively." (11) Employee Orientation—"I set up a program at one plant where we never had one." (12) Employee Development—"set up a program between workers and myself on development of their future and it has worked wonders." (13) Cost Management—"have cut down on unnecessary overtime, by about 60 percent." (14) Employee Relations—"I make it a practice to review my relationships with my employees daily. We have a good working relationship and I feel I have made great progress over the past six months to gain their trust."

Former participants also indicated reasons why they were not applying concepts from the program. Included were: already used the procedure, prefer using other procedures, not responsible for this area, am in a staff position, my supervisor or location will not allow it, and no current problem but will use it in the future.

The papers and discussion yield several conclusions about development of impact evaluation:

1. Evaluation is receiving increased attention from various disciplines such as instructional design, learning theory, economics, business, and industrial psychology.

2. Evaluation efforts have several goals: (1) to improve the quality of a management development program or (2) to develop evaluation *methods*.

3. It is important to monitor *all* influences on performance, *not* just program design, influences such as participant selection, management support, formal and informal communications about the program, organization support (or lack thereof) for target performance, and major events other than training that plausibly impact that performance. Admittedly this makes the evaluation job more complex, but it increases the probability of understanding *why* performance did or did not change and of modifying the conditions for performance change.

4. Evaluation itself can be a useful intervention. The decisions as to what to assess and the energy expended in assessing can lead to increased understanding of and focus on the performance.

5. A new type of validity was suggested. If an organization finds an activity valuable enough to support, it has proven itself to that organization. For people to *feel* that management development is worthwhile, the effects must be large enough to be seen and focused enough to be felt. Evaluation can help identify what is working and highlight supporting evidence.

The synergy and discussion at the conference suggest that it was worthwhile to the participants. Even partial answers to questions about evaluation purposes, procedures, and outcomes are encouraging. Evaluation conferences by ASTD and other associations in the field can be very useful to practitioners who seek to assess and improve the impact of continuing education. There is much work to be done.

references

Brethower, K. S., and Rummler, G. A. "Evaluating Training." *Improving Human Performance Quarterly,* 1976, 5 (3–4), 103–120.

Kirkpatrick, D. L. "Evaluation of Training." In R. L. Craig (Ed.), *Training and Development Handbook.* (2nd ed.). New York: McGraw-Hill, 1976.

McNamara, D. B., and Salinger, R. D. "Measuring the Payoff in Management Training." *Training and Development Journal,* April 1979, pp. 8–10.

Peterson, R. O. *Determining the Payoff of Management Training; A Series of Research Papers.* Madison, Wis.: American Society of Training and Development, 1979.

Karen Searles Brethower serves as vice-president for Managerial and Professional Development at the Chase Manhattan Bank N/A. She served as an expert observer at the conference and proposed strategies for improving impact evaluation studies.

*With the military spending millions of dollars annually on
literacy education, accurate evaluation of program
effectiveness is essential.*

evaluating military
literacy programs

gordon a. larson

The military has been one of the biggest sponsors of literacy education in
the United States since World War II. During both World Wars and
those in Korea and Vietnam, the military conducted massive literacy
programs to upgrade reading and math skills of undereducated service
personnel so that they could effectively participate in further military
training. The term "training" refers to instruction to increase proficiency to perform military tasks, in contrast to the term "education,"
which typically refers to voluntary training activities for self improvement outside military requirements. The military has also been involved
in peacetime literacy instruction as part of the Civilian Conservation
Corps (CCC) camp experience of the Depression and more recently in
support of the All Volunteer forces concept. With the exception of the
CCC experience, literacy education in the services has been conducted
primarily as part of the entry level instruction conducted at basic training centers. Its objective has been to raise general reading and math
proficiency to some predetermined grade level considered essential for
absorbing further military training. This level has ranged from fourth to

seventh grade over the years since World War II. Typically, recruits are given a reading test during processing, and those who fail to meet standards are sent to an intensive literacy program prior to entering some phase of the educational program (Goldberg, 1951; McGoff and Harding, 1974).

past evaluations of military literacy programs

As with most educational programs, effectiveness has normally been assessed on the basis of percentage of participants who achieve course graduation standards or of average grade level change of participants. These evaluation procedures can be integrated into the regular academic program with little or no additional resource requirements. However, these criteria are only intermediate indicators of program effectiveness and, on several occasions, the military has resorted to more extensive evaluation procedures to find out whether literacy instruction has had the desired effect on performance in subsequent training or on the job.

Although there were, reportedly, several attempts to assess literacy program effectiveness during World War II, the first fully documented studies came from Columbia University during the early 1950s. Goldberg (1951), Ginzberg and Bray (1953), and Hagen and Thorndike (1953) all used post hoc techniques to evaluate the effectiveness of the World War II program. They compared military records of program graduates with those of more literate soldiers and found that program graduates performed less well on most indexes of military proficiency. At the same time, they judged the program to be successful due to the overall satisfactory performance of program graduates. Post hoc procedures have the advantage of taking less time than longitudinal evaluations, but the lack of truly comparable control groups prevents one from predicting how participants would have performed without the intervening instruction. This method is also susceptible to problems of missing and inaccurate performance data, because data collection procedures are not specified in advance.

A variation of the post hoc evaluation procedure was used by Fisher (1971) to evaluate the effects of literacy instruction on performance in basic training. He compared the records of participants who achieved the fifth grade instructional goal with those who failed to achieve that standard and found no significant differences on most indexes of proficiency. A more effective method was employed by Goffard (1956) to evaluate literacy program effectiveness. He used experimental design procedures to compare training performance of participants in the program with an equivalent group of poor readers who did not participate. He also compared the performance of both of these groups against a selected group of normally literate trainees involved in basic training during the same period. Both the experimental and control groups performed less well than their more literate contemporaries on most indexes of training proficiency. Participants in literacy training performed slightly better than the control group on these same criteria.

The experimental design procedure is the most defensible impact evaluation method from a scientific perspective. It controls for most factors affecting internal validity and therefore provides the most scientifically reliable data. However, it is often difficult to employ this method because it requires control over the assignment of subjects to experimental and control groups and tends to disrupt normal instructional operations. Consequently, this procedure is not often employed in actual evaluations. In 1977, however, the author employed an experimental design to evaluate the effectiveness of the Army literacy program at Fort Dix, New Jersey (Larson, 1978, 1979). The program, the evaluation, and actions taken as a result of the evaluation are presented here to illustrate the requirements and potential benefits of this procedure.

the fort dix literacy program

The literacy program at Fort Dix in 1977 was conducted in accordance with a basic program model used at all five basic training centers in the Army at that time. Trainees were tested during processing, and those who scored below the 6.1 reading grade level were assigned to a six-week prevocational literacy program following basic training and prior to beginning occupational education. During this six-week period they were assigned to a special training company and attended reading and math classes seven hours per day, five days per week. Both general reading and job-related math and reading skills were taught. Over 2,000 trainees participated in the program during 1977 at an estimated cost of more than two million dollars. Most of the costs were related to support of the trainees for the six week period.

the evaluation procedure

The evaluation was conducted at the request of the deputy commander of Fort Dix, who was interested in finding out whether or not the program was cost-effective. His interest had been stimulated by the lack of accurate follow-up data on program graduates and questions concerning the relative performance of graduates who achieved program reading objectives and those who did not.

The basic evaluation design and procedures were developed over a three-month period through consultations with educational research experts, statisticians, and members of the military training establishment. In the final design, two major indicators of training performance were selected as dependent variables. These were attrition rate from occupational training and time required to complete occupational training successfully. These two variables are the major cost variables in training and thus the best indicators of cost-effectiveness.

The subjects were selected from more than 2,000 men assigned to Fort Dix for cooks, mechanics, and truckdrivers training between April and August of 1977. The regular program selection criterion of 6.1 reading grade level was used to select subjects for the study, but a different reading test was used to provide more accurate pretest and posttest data. A total of seventy-six men were selected for the experimental group and ninety-one for the control group.

Evaluation of trainee performance was based on procedures and records used in regular training courses. This facilitated the collection of data, and only one researcher was required on a half-time basis to collect, tabulate, and analyze the data. The total project took nine months from the start of initial testing to graduation of the last member of the experimental group. Data analysis was limited to application of chi-square and t-tests which could be calculated without the use of computers.

findings

When the study was completed in December of 1978, the results were surprising. Contrary to expectations, the control groups had no higher attrition rates than either the experimental group or the normal trainee population. In two of the three courses there were no significant differences in training times achieved by the experimental and control groups. Also, the average training times achieved by the marginal readers involved in the study did not differ significantly from those of the normal trainee population. The conclusion drawn from these findings was that general reading ability was not a significant factor in job training performance and was therefore not subject to remediation. A two-day average gain in training time achieved by program graduates in the mechanics course indicated, however, that literacy instruction did have some effect on training performance. Further analysis of data suggested that the effect was due to specific literacy skills attained in literacy training that were required in the job training course, such as use of forms and technical manuals.

These results demonstrated that the prevocational literacy instruction model could not be justified on a cost-effectiveness basis. At the same time, there was evidence that specific literacy instruction had a positive effect on training performance. This called for a redesign of the basic instructional model. If literacy instruction was not required prior to training, it could be conducted as an integral component of the normal training program at a greatly reduced cost. Elimination of the support costs alone would save nearly 85 percent of the total program costs, and by reducing the amount of general reading instruction the instructional staff could be reduced to about half the size.

resultant program changes

During the six months following completion of the evaluation, the literacy program was redesigned. The literacy course was to be integrated into the regular training program under the supervision of each training program director. Selection for literacy instruction was to be based on instructor referral or results of locally designed tests of specific literacy deficiencies, rather than reading grade levels. Since occupational training was self-paced, individuals could be withdrawn for short periods of time to provide them with the specific reading and math skills required at a given point in the job training program.

This instructional model was introduced in July 1978 and it produced several major benefits. First, it eliminated the support costs of literacy instruction. Second, the instruction was made more meaningful and was reinforced by relating it directly to the immediate literacy demands of training. Third, it reduced the amount of time spent in classroom instruction, which was appealing to the average marginal literate who had an aversion to the school environment to start with. Finally, it made use of the language experience gained in the training environment to develop the specific job-related vocabulary essential to comprehension.

Improvement in the literacy program at Fort Dix was made possible by the effective use of an appropriate evaluation technique which showed that literacy instruction did not have to be conducted prior to the start of occupational training. The evaluation design also allowed for a more accurate interpretation of actual program effects that pointed the way to specific program changes.

references

Fisher, A. H. *Army "New Standard" Personnel: Effect of Remedial Literacy Training on Performance in Military Service.* Alexandria, Va.: Air Force Human Resource Laboratory, 1971.

Ginzberg, E., and Bray, D. W. *The Uneducated.* New York: Columbia University Press, 1953.

Goffard, S. J. *An Experimental Evaluation of a Basic Education Program in the Army.* Washington, D.C.: Human Resources Research Organization, 1956.

Goldberg, S. *Army Training of Illiterates in World War II.* New York: Columbia University, Teachers College Press, 1951.

Hagen, E. P., and Thorndike, R. L. *A Study of World War II Navy Careers of Illiterates Sent through Literacy Training.* Washington, D.C.: Bureau of Naval Research, 1953.

Larson, G. A. "The Effects of Literacy Training on Performance in Occupational Training Programs in the U.S. Army." Unpublished doctoral dissertation, Rutgers University, 1979.

Larson, G. A. *Research on Literacy and Military Training: A Special Report to the Assistant Secretary of the Army.* Fort Dix, N.J.: Directorate of Personnel and Community Activities, 1978.

McGoff, R. M., and Harding, F. D. *A Report on Literacy Training Programs in the Armed Forces,* Alexandria, Va.: Air Force Human Resources Laboratory, 1974.

Gordon A. Larson is a Captain in the U.S. Army currently serving as chief of Basic Skills Education in the Directorate of Personnel and Community Activities at Fort Dix, New Jersey. He was recently appointed a research associate for the Center for Adult Development at Rutgers University, where he received his doctorate in adult education in 1979.

*Practitioners in continuing medical education should
evaluate the impact educational activities have on
physician competence, physician performance, or patient
health status.*

impact evaluation in continuing medical education— the missing link

joseph s. green
patrick l. walsh

The link between continuing medical education (CME) activities and the impact those programs have on the quality of health care is uncertain. Many factors contribute to this: (1) lack of adequate measures of physician performance or competence; (2) lack of sophisticated and creative educational measurement devices; (3) overreliance on CME to directly improve patient care; and (4) lack of commitment on the part of medical educators to apply the rigors of scientific inquiry to CME evaluation efforts (Abrahamson, 1968). Another factor, common to all educational fields, is the lack of effective communication between practitioners and researchers as both attempt to solve real-world problems utilizing knowledge resources (Knox, 1976).

A glaring weakness of continuing professional education (CPE), is its failure to document the nature of its effect on professional services

(Pennington and Green, 1976). CPE activities often fail to adequately assess specific deficiencies in professional practice, and fail to evaluate the reduction of these deficiencies as well.

The Focus and Purpose. This chapter will focus on CME impact studies primarily in the hospital setting. Accountability in medical care practice is demanded from many quarters. The hospital setting appears to offer some necessary controls on the quality of practice and, therefore, on the potential for impact studies. Malpractice suits, withholding privileges to practice, mandatory peer review sessions, staff development activities, and patient care audit all require the individual physician to be accountable to himself, his peers, his employers (in the hospital), and the public.

Whenever appropriate, existing sources of information should be utilized. Patient care audits utilizing medical records are now mandated for hospitals to receive accreditation by the Joint Commission on Accreditation of Hospitals. Utilization review studies are also mandated. These reports include data on utilization of resources, drug utilization, and typical lengths of stay. Morbidity and mortality conferences and tissue committees provide data on specific problem areas in direct patient care. Recidivism rates are also available in many hospitals, especially in the areas of substance abuse, mental health, and chronic physical diseases or disabilities. Hospital administrators also collect critical incident reports which might provide data to make judgments about the impact of educational interventions. Many hospitals have also recently instigated patient satisfaction surveys that provide another source.

In addition to existing data sources, individuals within the health care setting should be considered as valuable data sources. Physicians, other health care providers, administrators, supervisors, patients, and families of patients each have unique perspectives.

Considering all potential data sources, decisions on which sources to use should be made based on some of the following: (1) availability of data; (2) relevance of data to the issue at hand (validity); (3) reliability of the data source; (4) availability of methods to collect those data; (5) the degree to which the data collection methods intrude; (6) the trade-offs between effort expended and information yielded; and (7) resources available for the study.

When possible, multiple data sources should be used. As attempts are made to better understand the nature of impact, it is extremely helpful to look at many relevant sources (within budget and time limitations). Where data all agree, one can feel reasonably assured that an accurate picture has been drawn. This process of data "triangulation"

(Webb, 1970) adds immeasurably to the credibility of impact data. Although there are obvious strengths associated with the use of more objective data, care should be taken not to totally dismiss subjective perceptions. It is important to understand the strengths and weaknesses of each type of data and combine sources that maximize strengths and minimize weaknesses.

For any particular data source, there are also a variety of methods by which those data might be gathered. Methods to evaluate physician-student performance in CME include: (1) paper and pencil instruments —to determine cognitive gain or attitude change; (2) observational checklists or rating scales—to ascertain skill development or changes in performance; and (3) questionnaires, surveys, or interviews—to obtain perceptions on processes, attitudes, or behavior changes. As impact or change in physician performance becomes the focus, review of medical records and other existing data on patient care become more important. However, the real weakness in all CME evaluation has been the inability of impact studies to draw any definitive relationships between discovered behavior change and the CME activity. "The weakness of most published evaluations limit possible conclusions about the effectiveness of CME" (Bertram and Brooks-Bertram, 1977, p. 330).

New measurement techniques have been developed within the past fifteen years. Some of these include: (1) videotaping and use of motion pictures for documenting and testing performance; (2) erasure techniques in testing clinical skills; (3) simulation methods for assessing diagnostic skills; and (4) the substitution of nonpatients for real ones to facilitate testing of clinical performance (Abrahamson, 1968).

What is needed in the future is threefold: (1) health care researchers should continue to analyze the relationship between health care processes and patient care outcomes (Williamson, 1971); (2) continuing medical educators should begin to describe relationships between CME activities and health care processes (physician competence and performance) (Williamson, and others, 1967; Williamson, 1971); and (3) those involved in CME should utilize all of the technology and measurement techniques available to discern changes in physician performance.

CME impact studies

Some impact studies on CME have attempted to link education and performance. Four major works summarized those attempts. Bertram and Brooks-Bertram (1977) reviewed published CME evaluation reports for the years 1960 through 1977. They stated that evaluation designs providing the strongest assurances of valid results involve comparison groups, and these are uncommon in the bulk of CME evaluations. While more than one variable was studied in many of the evaluations they summarized, no attempt was made in any study to correlate two or more of the variables. "It should be informative to know if indeed those physicians who changed their behavior after a CME program were the same or different from those who improved on a knowledge test or expressed favorable opinions" (Bertram and Brooks-Bertram, 1977, p. 344). One CME impact evaluation report (Richardson, Green, and Shew, 1976) did attempt to correlate changes in attitudes, cognitive gain scores, and follow-up self-reported behavior change. The principal finding was that those who improved practice by changing behavior were those who had *both* significantly increased their knowledge and significantly improved their attitudes.

A second review done by Lloyd and Abrahamson (1977) reviewed the effectiveness of CME activities in terms of their impact on physician competence, performance, and patient health status. Twenty-two studies looked at CME's impact on competence (ten studies indicating a statistically significant improvement); twenty-six studied the impact on performance (eleven indicating some improvement); and four studies aimed at patient health status (two demonstrating significant improvement). However, of the twenty-three studies indicating positive relationships between CME and indicators of impact, only five studies were designed in a way to account for possible intervening or contaminating variables.

The third review was accomplished by the Association of American Medical Colleges (Waddell, 1978). The relevant sections in that document looked at physicians' diligence in utilizing knowledge and skills and physicians' motivation to utilize CME results. The implications drawn from this effort focused on conditions under which CME activities were likely to impact on physicians' behavior. The findings from a multitude of studies indicated that CME must: (1) be closely tied in time to an individual patient care event; (2) have personal consequences for the physician; (3) get the physician's attention; (4) be related to patient health care problems perceived as being severe by the physician; (5) be initiated by peer review in accordance with agreed-upon criteria ("bicycle approach"; Brown and Fleischer, 1971); or (6) be focused on an area of high interest (for example, cost) to the physician.

Another review was conducted by Nakamoto and Verner (1973) on continuing education in the health professions. Their conclusions regarding impact evaluation in CME were succinctly stated: "This review of studies on evaluation has found a general lack of substantive research and can but repeat the discouraging conclusion of many writers in the field that CME may not be having a demonstrable effect on medical care" (Nakamoto and Verner, p. 143). The critical phrases are "substantive research" and "demonstrable effect"; the major implication for all educators in CME is to further develop our capacities to do the former so that some day we may convincingly show the latter.

In order to provide practitioners with more in-depth information on several creative approaches to impact evaluation, the next section will give descriptions of two such studies.

Case Studies. Brown and Uhl (1970) reported on efforts at Chestnut Hill Community Hospital to conduct a number of evaluations which produced promising results. In one study, ten prevalent diseases were identified. The hospital staff treating each of these disease entities developed criteria for evaluating performance in the management of these high priority diseases. Using these criteria in conjunction with chart reviews and patient follow-ups, Brown and his group were able to demonstrate the value of this approach in arriving at precise objectives by which educational efforts could be measured in behavioral terms. To illustrate, they report an investigation conducted in the use of antibiotics: "From studies of those health problems which the system of priority indicated as offering significant potentialities for improving patient care, it became evident that since in one medical department a review of fifty consecutive records of patients revealed only a thirty percent correct usage of antibiotics, a program was required to correct the educational deficit" (Brown and Uhl, 1970, p. 1664).

To determine whether the educational deficit in this case was an informational or problem solving deficiency, an examination based on sixteen of the cases reviewed was taken by forty-two members of the department studied. The test results indicated physicians had adequate knowledge, so four conferences were held in which the physicians discussed patient management (problem solving) with experts and appropriate literature was introduced when necessary. A follow-up study on the performance of physicians, using chart reviews and data from the pharmacy, revealed changes in drug use and management practices consistent with the behavioral change desired.

There have also been several attempts to help physicians identify their own deficiencies based on patient care research and then to evaluate the effect of educational efforts designed to help overcome these deficiencies. One study using this approach was reported by Williamson and others (1968). The purposes of this project were to: (1) measure physicians' responses to abnormal and unexpected results of three routine admission tests; (2) ascertain whether the physicians needed to improve their responses; (3) provide the required education; (4) reassess responses to these screening tests; and (5) evaluate and repeat the cycle as many times as required to achieve and measure the desired level of proficiency. Initial assessment was accomplished by means of a chart review and, since it revealed that approximately two-thirds of the unexpected abnormal test results went unheeded, a workshop was held to discuss the findings. Although a subjective evaluation of the workshop indicated that the physicians found it stimulating and informative, follow-up chart reviews disclosed continued neglect of laboratory reports. Accordingly, the educational approach was changed with efforts directed toward altering the physicians' behavioral patterns. Removable fluorescent tape was used to obscure abnormal data on the laboratory reports. This resulted in a significant improvement in the physicians' response to test results. This change in behavior was maintained by more than one-half of the participants six months after the use of the tape was discontinued.

conclusions and summary

The "Missing Link" in continuing medical education is evidence of the impact of CME activities on physician proficiency, physician performance, or patient health status. Educational practitioners in CME settings and health researchers must together analyze relationships among the relevant activities and outcomes. Continuing medical education activities are not in and of themselves sufficient to justify present or projected expenditures. Physicians, CME practitioners, and the public must become convinced of their value in improving the quality of health care. Toward that goal, a rededication is needed.

references

Abrahamson, S. "Evaluation in Continuing Medical Education." *Journal of the American Medical Association (JAMA)*, 1968, *206* (3), 625–628.

Bertram, D., and Brooks-Bertram, P. "The Evaluation of Continuing Medical Education: A Literature Review." *Health Education Monographs*, 1977, *5* (4), 330–362.

Brown, C., and Fleischer, D. "The Bi-Cycle Concept—Relating Continuing Education Directly to Patient Care." In N. S. Stearns and others (Eds.), *Continuing Medical Education in Community Hospitals: A Manual for Program Development*. Boston, Mass.: Postgraduate Medical Institute, 1971.

Brown, C., and Uhl, H. "Mandatory Continuing Education: Sense or Non-Sense." *JAMA*, 1970, *213*, 1660–1668.

Knox, A. "Helping Adults to Learn." Washington, D.C.: Continuing Library Education Network and Exchange, 1976.

Lloyd, J., and Abrahamson, S. *Effectiveness of Continuing Medical Education—A Review of the Evidence*. Presentation at the Council of Medical Specialty Societies, Scottsdale, Ariz., February 1977.

Nakamoto, J., and Verner, C. *Continuing Education in the Health Professions: A Review of the Literature—1960-70*. Syracuse, N.Y.: The ERIC Clearinghouse on Adult Education, 1973.

Pennington, F., and Green, J. "Continuing Professional Education: A Comparative Analysis of the Program Development Process in Six Professions." *Adult Education*, 1976, *27* (1), 13–23.

Richardson, G., Green, J., and Shew, R. *Sexual Health and the Health Care Professional—An Evaluation of Impact*. Salt Lake City, Utah: InterWest Regional Medical Education Center, VA Medical Center, 1976.

Waddell, W. "Profile #2. Continuing Medical Education—Data for Modeling." Background paper for AAMC Modeling Project, August, 1978.

Webb, E. "Unconventionality, Triangulation, and Inference." In N. Denzin (Ed.), *Sociologist Methods*. Chicago: Aldine, 1970.

Williamson, J. "Evaluating Quality of Patient Care: A Strategy Relating Outcome and Process Assessment." *JAMA*, 1971, *218* (4), 564–569.

Williamson, J., and others. "Continuing Education and Patient Care Research." *JAMA*, 1967, *201* (12), 118–122.

Williamson, J., and others. "Priorities in Patient Care Research and Continuing Medical Education." *JAMA*, 1968, *204*, 93–98.

Joseph S. Green, Ph.D., has been associated with the InterWest Regional Medical Education Center at the Salt Lake City VA Medical Center since 1975; initially as the coordinator, Instructional Design and Evaluation and subsequently as codirector. He has recently accepted a position as Educational Director of the Foundation for Continuing Medical Education, located in Fresno, California.

Patrick L. Walsh, M.A., has been with the Regional Medical Education Centers in Minneapolis and Salt Lake City, serving as coordinator of Educational Evaluation in Minneapolis and assistant director in Salt Lake City.

A new methodology was used to measure the impact of a simulation workshop on job behaviors of adult education administrators who demonstrated significant changes ten months after their in-service experience.

in-service education— does it make a difference?

doe hentschel

Continuing education programs for educators are not markedly different today from those conducted in the early 1900s, yet the bulk of available literature indicates that we know very little about the results of in-service education. Rather than assessing whether or not changes in performance became integrated into the normal work patterns of participants, most evaluations are based on self-report data about how satisfied participants were with the experience or how much they believe they were affected by or will change as a result of the program.

An extensive review of evaluations of in-service programs (Hentschel, 1977) yielded very few evaluations that examined the impact of such programs. Mayer, Disinger, and White (1975) evaluated a National Science Foundation program for earth science teachers, and their report is one of the few that meets sound evaluation criteria. The educational program which they evaluated included a four-week summer workshop in 1969, trainee observation of pilot classes and monthly review meetings throughout the 1969–70 school year, and a six-week summer session followed by implementation of earth science courses by the trainees with monthly review meetings during 1970–71. The evaluators used pre- and post-training content examinations to assess participants' knowledge and understanding of earth science, examinations given to students over three years to assess their cognitive growth, and a teacher behavior checklist completed by the students to assess changes in teacher classroom performance. Results were positive: significant gains in knowledge of students and teachers were achieved; and greater gains were made in performance change by teachers who participated both years. Their conclusion was that:

> A program focusing on the role of the teacher in the classroom, utilizing those materials and methods which the teacher is expected to use, is effective in changing teacher behavior toward more inquiry-oriented approaches, concurrent with increasing the teachers' information base and understanding of relevant concepts. It also indicates that such changes in teaching behavior persist at least one year beyond the termination of the program (Mayer, Disinger, and White, 1975, p. 152).

This extensive educational program demonstrates the use of many useful concepts of planned change including clear program objectives so participants knew expectations, considerable time to transmit knowledge, followed by a vicarious trial. Continued information, support, and interaction were provided during the confirmation stage of the change process when the trainees were experimenting with the new methods. Such support is considered critical in terms of long-term adoption and is rarely present in most typical in-service programs.

simulation as a technique

While most evaluation reports of in-service education programs focus on the continuing education of teachers, the professional development of administrators is no less important. One of the few relatively new techniques employed in pre- and in-service education of educational administrators is simulation using activities such as case studies, in-basket exercises, and role playing.

Greenlaw, Herron, and Rowdon (1962) credit the wide acceptance and use of simulation to the method's inherent characteristics which are consistent with current adult learning theory. They cite the intense involvement of participants, the illusion of reality that demands a total rather than fragmented response, the relevance of the learning, the opportunity for trial practice of the new skills, and the reinforcement provided by reaction to the learners. According to Cunningham (1971) simulation is the most promising, currently available, single innovation in administrator preparation, yet measuring the impact of these methods on those who are exposed to them is one of the most critical unresolved issues in the incorporation of simulated approaches in more traditional educational programs.

a simulation for adult educators

In a recently completed study (Hentschel, 1979), the author designed a simulation workshop for continuing education administrators and assessed the impact of the learning experience on their job behaviors. The workshop was sponsored by the Adult Education Service Center serving metropolitan Chicago. This Center, a federally funded project administered by Northern Illinois University, is one of six in the State designed to upgrade the adult education delivery system through staff development, curriculum and materials development and evaluation, and dissemination of resources to continuing education practitioners.

The objective of the simulation workshop was to teach the processes of program evaluation, as developed by the Center for the Study of Evaluation (CSE) at UCLA, so that the participants (who were practicing administrators in a wide variety of adult and continuing education programs) would be able to function more effectively in their own programs in the design and implementation of evaluative processes. The principles of continuing education, group process, and planned change served as theoretical bases upon which the workshop was designed. It was conducted on one evening and two full days with a total of fifteen instructional hours divided into five three-hour modules. Each module consisted of a slide-tape providing background information on a task to be completed by teams of four or five participants, and a reaction segment in which each team shared its product and all were compared to a standard response. The five sequential modules involved participants in the entire evaluation process, from needs assessment of program goals through formulating an administrative response to a summative evaluation report, in a "slice of life" fashion.

evaluating the workshop

The primary focus of the impact evaluation of the workshop was to find out whether or not those who participated actually used the evaluation techniques from the simulation in their jobs. The problems associated with such evaluations include the need to go beyond self-report data and to actually observe performance of participants on the job. Such observation, particularly as follow-up evaluation some time after the program has been completed, is generally considered to be unfeasible by evaluators and researchers. To resolve these problems, a new methodology was devised and piloted for this study.

The "Verified" Interview. Trained interviewers conducted "verified" personal interviews with participants prior to the workshop and then ten months later. An inventory of nine specific behaviors or techniques that were included in the content of the workshop served as an instrument to score the responses to the structured interview schedule. The schedule was constructed so that information about each behavior could be solicited without directly asking the interviewees whether or not they performed the desired behaviors. Whenever interviewees reported a desired behavior, the interviewer asked them if they could show an example of what they did. Since the interviews were conducted in the interviewees' offices, they had ready access to files, promotional literature, and other documents that could be used for verification.

The atmosphere created by the interviewer was friendly and nonthreatening. It was explained that, in the case of the pretest interview, information was being solicited for the purpose of ascertaining the specific needs of the workshop participants and assessing their current practices. In the posttest interview, emphasis was placed on assessing the effectiveness of the workshop as opposed to "testing" the skill level of those who had participated. Most interviewees responded favorably to the tone set in the interview and were not only willing to share artifacts that served to verify their behaviors, but frequently did so even without being asked. It was not unusual, however, for an interviewee to respond to a question by mentioning a particular practice (for example, "We survey our students") but, when asked to share it be unable to produce an example. Thus a scoring scheme was developed which, while not discounting unverified behaviors, clearly weighted scores in favor of verified activity. The scale used was: Regular, verified performance—3; Occasional, verified performance—2; Unverified performance—1; No indication of performance—0. In addition, 1 point was earned for each separate type of needs assessment activity and for each specific method of collecting formative evaluation data. Thus, with nine behaviors on the inventory, scores could range from 0–27+ points. Coded interview reports were scored by both the interviewer and the evaluator, and the mean score was used in the data analysis (see Table 1).

Table 1. Selected Items from Interview Schedule and Behaviors Inventory

Interview	Inventory (Desired Behavior)	Typical Artifacts Produced
How do you decide what to include in a program or course?	Conducts needs assessements	Surveys, Student Assessments, Advisory Committee Minutes
Who decides what should be accomplished in these programs? Is this information spelled out clearly?	Formulates written objectives	Course syllabi, Catalogues, Promotional literature
Have you ever actually measured the final results of a program?	Has conducted outcome evaluations by self, other in house evaluator, or outside evaluator	Evaluation reports, Statistical summaries, State reports

Data Analysis. The pre- and post-test scores of workshop participants were compared with pre- and post-test scores of a control group. The control group consisted of people who had indicated an interest in taking the workshop and were interviewed but who subsequently failed to register for the program.

The control group (n=10) experienced a slight, nonsignificant decline in their use of evaluation techniques as measured by the verified interview from a mean score of 15.6 to a mean of 14.1. The treatment group (n=20) experienced an increase from 12.27 to 16.02. A t-test on the differences between the means resulted in a t value of 2.978, significant at less than the .005 level with 19 degrees of freedom (one-tailed probability). Fifteen members of this group raised their scores, two remained the same, and three declined.

Interpretation of the Findings. The simulation workshop did result in changed performance among participants. Ten months after the workshop, they were using evaluation techniques that had not been part of their normal administrative repertoire prior to the simulation experience. Although the sample size in the study was small, with twenty in the experimental group and ten in the control group, such numbers are typical of in-service activities. The conclusion about the effectiveness of the workshop and its impact on participants' performance, while not subject to broad generalization, is a meaningful statement about the impact of this particular continuing education experience on this particular group of continuing education administrators.

The use of the *verified* pre- and post-test interview appears to be a feasible methodology for assessing on-the-job administrative performance. Approximately thirty minutes were required for each interview, and because in most cases the number of in-service participants is relatively small, this method does make evaluation of impact possible. Continuing education program planners could reasonably include verified interviews of potential participants among their needs assessment activities in early stages of program development. Repeating these interviews at various intervals after completion of the program would provide both impact evaluation data and ongoing needs assessment.

In conclusion, it should be noted that the subject matter of the simulation workshop designed for this study was selected because of the critical need for training in evaluation techniques for continuing education administrators. The effectiveness of this training program in particular and of simulation as a training methodology in general might indicate future directions for more massive efforts to improve proficiency in this important area.

references

Cunningham, L. "A Powerful But Underdeveloped Educational Tool." In D. L. Bolton (Ed.), *The Use of Simulation in Educational Administration.* Columbus, Ohio: Merrill, 1971.

Greenlaw, P. S., Herron, L. N., and Rowdon, R. *Business Simulation in Industrial and University Education.* Englewood Cliffs, N.J.: Prentice-Hall, 1962.

Hentschel, D. "Change Theory Applied to In-Service Education." *Planning and Changing,* 1977, *8* (2), 103–114.

Hentschel, D. "The Development and Utilization of a Simulation Workshop as a Strategy for Changing Job Behaviors of Adult Education Administrators." Unpublished doctoral dissertation, University of Wisconsin-Milwaukee, 1979.

Mayer, V. J., Disinger, J. F., and White, A. L. "Evaluation of an In-Service Program for Earth Science Teachers." *Science Education,* 1975, 59 (April-June), 146–152.

Doe Hentschel is the Regional Program Director for Continuing Education and Public Service in Chicago for the University of Illinois. She has served as a consultant in program development and administrative leadership to numerous institutions and organizations.

Some evaluations appear to be inexpensive, but when all
factors are accounted for, there are few bargains.

cost-effective evaluation:
is there a $500 solution
for a $1000 problem?

dale rusnell

Formal evaluation of outcomes is omitted or receives cursory treatment
in most continuing education programs. It is neglected when educational practitioners feel that evaluation requires complex technical
knowledge, or that informal response and personal observation are sufficient. It is also neglected when administrators feel that evaluation
wastes time and resources that could be spent in other ways. This chapter focuses on the administrator's concern to ensure that benefits outweigh costs of doing an evaluation of program impact.

    Evaluation costs are controllable. For both small and large pro-
grams, impact evaluations can vary widely in scope and cost. Ten percent
of total program costs is sometimes suggested for use in evaluation.
Some form of evaluation is possible within almost any program budget.
Ten dollars may procure appropriate information concerning the impact of some programs. However, spending too little may not provide
sufficient information and spending too much may provide unneeded

information. A first concern in controlling costs is that resources be used efficiently so that fair value is obtained from all expenditures. A second concern is that resources be used effectively so that objectives are reached at an acceptable cost. Evaluations may be cost-efficient by using resources sparingly for the work done, but to be cost-effective, evaluations must attempt to reach objectives with neither too little nor too much effort.

Knowledge about both objectives and costs is needed to assess cost-effectiveness. Objectives for evaluation arise from a clear understanding about the intended audiences and purposes for which information will be used. Given a set of objectives for the particular purposes of a specific audience, cost-effectiveness of alternative evaluation strategies may be compared. In such a comparison, at least four types of cost should be considered: (1) dollar expenditures (salaries, equipment, travel); (2) indirect expenditures (depreciation on equipment, value of space allocation); (3) other quantifiable factors (time of learners used to obtain data); (4) other nonquantifiable factors (changes in morale of staff and participants) (Popham, 1975). Cost-effective impact evaluation attempts to provide essential information for specific evaluation objectives, taking into account implications of all four types of cost.

fundamental issues affecting costs

Sources of evaluation cost are obvious: salaries, travel, equipment, facilities, materials, and services. Underlying those sources, however, are some fundamental issues affecting cost. Ultimate costs result from the choice of an evaluation plan, which in turn reflects characteristics of the program to be examined as well as the purposes of evaluation. Evaluation costs are affected by the nature and size of the program, the degree of contingency interpretation desired for program outcomes, and the degree of proof required to establish causal links between the program and outcomes found among participants. Each of these three features is elaborated below.

Characteristics of the Program. Basic strategies for evaluation depend on the nature of programs. Evaluating attitudinal outcomes can be inherently more costly than evaluating informational outcomes. Evaluating complex learning results may be more costly than examining simple learning. Types of participants may affect costs as well, because some participants are more difficult to communicate with or gain cooperation from. Design of the program may also affect costs, as the scheduling of times, locations, and topics may affect observation procedures used in the evaluation.

As program size increases with respect to number of participants, extent of geographical area, and number of separate events, costs of evaluation rise. Intuitively, costs for assessing a one-week workshop should be less than those for a national literacy program. When participant numbers increase, costs for materials, data collection, and data processing are greater. When geographical areas and number of events expand, additional staff, facilities, equipment, and communication costs may be required.

Program evaluation costs may be either fixed or variable in nature. In terms of line budgets, fixed costs such as salaries, equipment, and facilities remain stable and independent of the volume of assessment activity required, over reasonable ranges of program size. Variable costs such as travel, materials, postage, and data processing increase gradually with the volume of activities. Thus, for programs of 100 and 500 participants, fixed costs may be similar but variable costs will differ. Similarly, in terms of performance budgets, designing the evaluation, developing instruments, and writing final reports remain stable over ranges of program size, while data collection and data analysis increase in cost with the size of the program.

For any evaluation, a basic fixed cost exists for personnel and other assets that are required. Once those resources are contracted for, fixed costs are not easily adjusted. Variable costs are more easily changed on short notice. It is easier to reduce materials and travel costs than to reduce salary and benefit costs. Cost-effectiveness is achieved by ensuring that fixed costs are fully employed and that variable costs are used efficiently. When the nature and size of a program is considered, it is desirable to select an evaluation strategy that uses fixed resources fully. Cost-effectiveness is lowered when additional resources such as an additional staff member or another office are required to conduct the evaluation, but the full potential productivity of those resources is not needed. Part-time staff and shared resources can be used to maintain the cost-effectiveness level in those cases.

Degree of Contingency Interpretation Desired. Stake's Countenance Model (1967) suggests that results are contingent upon a set of logical relationships among program rationale, inputs, processes, and outcomes. Evaluation costs are affected by the degree to which those relationships need to be described and interpreted. For some purposes, such as providing certification for legal requirements, only the final outcomes are of concern. For other purposes, such as identifying reasons for success or failure, interpretation of the contingency relationships is necessary.

Whenever full understanding of the positive and negative judgments inherent in evaluation is required, a broader base of information is necessary than might be collected only at a program's conclusion. Stufflebeam (1973) suggests that good summative evaluation depends upon good formative information. Interpretation of conclusions can involve analysis of the contingencies, identification of discrepancies between intents and observations, clarification of criteria and standards for making judgments, or assessment of consistency for data gathered from various groups. Monetary implications for collecting those types of information are clear: additional time and resources are needed to collect additional data.

Evaluations that collect data only at the conclusion of a program may be inexpensive, but the potential for interpreting the findings will likely be small. In cost-effectiveness terms, greater expenses required to raise the potential for interpretation of outcomes can be a worthwhile investment, because a minimal-cost procedure may be a total waste of resources if the required data are not created. Costs of collecting data for interpretation are of benefit only if the information is used to advantage for the objectives of evaluation. Controlling those expenses is possible by assessing the degree of interpretation desired. Inexpensive impact evaluation can be done more easily when objectives do not require contingency interpretations.

Degree of Proof Desired to Establish Program Effectiveness. Continuing education programs attempt to promote change through learning. When outcomes are assessed, decision makers may accept various levels of evidence to establish that a change has occurred among participants and that the program was a direct cause of those changes. Factors exist which, if not accounted for in evaluation, may cause difficulty in proving beyond doubt either that the change occurred or that the cause of the change was the program. Alternative explanations include the possibilities that results may be due to other events in the lives of its participants (historical events in society or human maturation), that results may be related to the nature or use of observation instruments (technical aspects of measurement instruments or experience with repeated use of identical tests), or that participant groups are unique in some way that affects the interpretation of outcomes (extreme differences among comparison groups or extreme original performances which naturally move toward an average) (Popham, 1975). Proof of program effectiveness relies on eliminating such alternatives as potential explanations for the outcomes.

To interpret results it is desirable to show that a change has occurred among learners with respect to their knowledge, attitudes, skills, or behavior in societal settings. Normally, at least two observations are required to indicate change. One is suggested before the program and the other may be immediately following the program, at intermediate time periods, or after substantial time lags (Warr, Bird, and Rackham, 1970). In addition to charting changes among learners, influences over those changes may be interpreted. As observation moves further away from the program environment into other settings, it is more difficult to attribute changes to the program because the number of potential causes for change increases. It is also possible to assess the impacts of a program by examining the ultimate effects of participants' changed behavior over time, but proving the causes of those changes is difficult. Showing that increased profit for a company is directly connected to educational programs and the effects of changed employee behavior from those programs can be complex and expensive.

Where greater degrees of proof are required to establish program effectiveness, greater costs are incurred. Research designs that control or account for alternative explanations of change usually include multiple observations and use of control groups for comparison. As Kirkpatrick (1977) points out, it may not be worth the additional costs to obtain proof beyond doubt, so decision makers have the option of accepting lesser degrees of proof at lower cost, along with lower probabilities that the program was truly the cause of outcomes.

cost-controlling decisions in evaluation

Numerous decisions are necessary to plan and conduct any evaluation. The set of decisions comprising an evaluation may be visualized as a pyramid, with a few major decisions at the top of the structure and increasing numbers of less important decisions at lower levels. Decisions near the top affect larger numbers of subsequent decisions, and some decisions at lower levels cannot be made until the upper level decisions which control overall directions of an evaluation are made.

Most evaluations can be conducted in a variety of ways, each at a different cost. Since choices at the top of the pyramid establish important strategies and direction, they can control major elements of cost.

Grotelueschen and others (1974) suggest eight major components of any evaluation: purposes, audiences, issues, resources, evidence, data gathering, analysis, and reporting. If it is assumed that purposes and audiences are known and reflected in the evaluation objectives, the evaluator is faced with direction-setting decisions in each of the remaining six components. Some of those decisions will be examined briefly to identify their effects upon costs.

Issues. When considering the questions for evaluation to address, the degree to which assessment will focus on program goals affects cost. Outcome evaluation has traditionally been concerned with examining achievement of goals, but other options are available. Examination of side effects and unanticipated consequences is sometimes suggested, as is the goal-free approach. Costs are likely to increase whenever the focus moves beyond a set of specific, known goals. Because unintended outcomes are often unpredictable, a searching process is necessary to identify them, and because goal-free evaluation begins with no preconception of what outcomes to search for, a similar search is needed. Active searching for possible outcomes implies additional effort and resources beyond those needed to examine previously identified goals. Increased efforts may be offset by additional information to aid in assessing overall outcomes and impacts, but the issue demands attention as a cost-controlling decision.

Resources. An important resource and a major element of cost is the evaluator or the evaluation team. Costs for external evaluators are easily seen as direct expenses specified by contract. Internal evaluators are more often connected with indirect or opportunity costs. Budgeting for external evaluators can be straightforward, as costs may be precise and specific. Internal evaluators, however, may be seconded from other tasks so that no direct, specific costs are budgeted. True costs then depend upon the value of alternative activities left undone, or done with less efficiency by replacement staff. Use of internal work reassignment for evaluation may appear to be inexpensive since a direct budget line may not be needed, but true costs require careful analysis if this decision is to be used as a cost-controlling factor.

A second resource in evaluation includes all those participants, staff, administrators, and interested observers who may be called upon to provide information or to assist in other ways. Traditionally, evaluation has used those groups as passive providers of information. More recently, their active involvement in all phases of evaluation has been suggested to make the process more meaningful, useful, and responsive to needs of people throughout the program. Costs increase with active participation of program-related individuals, mainly in terms of lost opportunity and indirect costs. For active involvement by those individuals, time allocations may increase substantially for some activities such as planning and decision making, or may decrease for other phases such as data collection. Small amounts of time contributed by large numbers of people can significantly affect the true costs of an evaluation. However, benefits may also increase in nonquantifiable areas such as morale and enthusiasm. The relative effects, though difficult to measure, clearly warrant consideration in examining the total cost-effectiveness of evaluation.

Evidence. Research designs provide a plan for the number of observations to be made as well as the number of groups to be examined. Some major issues concerning research designs include whether control groups will be used, whether people should be selected randomly for groups, which groups are appropriate for comparison, and whether identical measurement instruments should be used repeatedly. Technical arguments concerning those issues focus on ensuring that measures of change are valid rather than artifacts of the instruments themselves, and ensuring that alternative explanations for outcomes are minimized. Typical designs include the one-group pretest-posttest, pretest-posttest control group, and interrupted time series (Campbell and Stanley, 1966). Costs of evaluation increase as the number of observations or the number of groups to be observed increases. The most common design used in evaluation is the one-shot case study, requiring only one observation of one group. It is not recommended where interpretation is desired for either change or causes of change. It does permit collection of participant reactions, which is perhaps the least expensive form of outcome evaluation. Selection of a research design is a major factor in cost control, because many evaluation activities arise from the design chosen. The design must allow for the interpretations desired, but should also consider cost. Finding the most cost-effective design is difficult and involves seeking a balance between an ideal design for the purposes and practical constraints imposed by program circumstances and budget.

Data Gathering. The essence of evaluation is assessing the value, merit, or worth of a program. That valuing process requires collection of information including descriptions of what was intended and what was observed, together with criteria and standards upon which judgments will be made. Competing value systems are often in conflict over criteria or standards, and evaluation costs increase as more information from different sources is needed to complete the valuing process.

Personal and nonpersonal sources of information may be used in evaluation. Information may be sought from a variety of people connected with the program, and documents, artifacts, or other program products may be examined. Where the number of information units for any source is large, sampling may be needed to control costs. In turn, sample size may be reduced to control costs so long as it is large enough for analytic purposes. Where the amount of information requested from individuals is large, different questions may be used with different individuals in multiple-matrix sampling procedures.

Evaluation costs may be controlled by the judicious selection of observation instruments and procedures. Interviews can be expensive when travel, repeat calls, and advanced phoning are considered. Telephone surveys or mailed questionnaires may be less expensive. Direct costs may be budgeted where commercial products are appropriate. Where instruments need to be developed, both direct and indirect costs are involved, including salaries and time for instrument validation. Those costs may be considerable. Because instrument development is a fixed cost, it can be difficult to justify for small projects because the cost per observation becomes very expensive. In practice, costs are reduced by eliminating sophisticated pilot-testing and validation activities.

Analysis. Data analysis must suit the type of information collected and also the purposes of evaluation. Both numeric and verbal operations are part of evaluation and costs are connected with each. Numeric analysis can require significant time for planning the strategy so that technical aspects of analysis are correct and all evaluation questions are appropriately answered. Preparing raw data for computation by hand or computer, and interpreting results obtained from summaries or tests also demands time and effort. Verbal analysis requires time to sort through comments, develop schemes to summarize information, and create generalizations about findings. In general, analysis procedures should match the precision of the data obtained. Analyzing gross estimates with high degrees of precision can be an unrecognized and inappropriate expense. While computer analysis appears inexpensive for the amount of data generated, time is required for interpretation of its results. The choice of analysis strategies is also determined by the purposes of evaluation. Numeric operations can provide precise comparisons and statistical tests, but verbal analyses can provide valuable suggestions or ideas to aid interpretation of the findings. Data analysis is cost-effective only if it provides essential information for evaluation purposes.

Reporting. Evaluations are normally conducted for specific reasons and specific audiences. The nature of reports required by audiences affects costs. Where the number of intended audiences is small, or the number of separate reports is limited, costs are reduced. Major costs connected with reporting are the time for writing reports and the duplicating of copies. Situations which demand a number of interim or specialized reports increase time costs, and situations which demand large volume mailings or reports increase duplicating and postage costs. Travel for personal reports at hearings or audiovisual presentations can raise costs significantly.

toward cost-effectiveness

Practical guidelines for designing cost-effective impact evaluation are difficult to suggest without considering specific circumstances of an evaluation. Each evaluation strategy includes direct and indirect costs and, as alternative strategies are compared, both types of cost should be considered. Trading direct, budgeted costs for indirect, unbudgeted costs does not make evaluation more cost-effective, although it may change the administrator's accountability level. Decision makers are sometimes less considerate of indirect costs such as time contributed by participants than they are of line budget items when they are not directly accountable for the indirect items. Ideally, evaluation should be done with minimal direct as well as indirect costs. Enthusiasm for this ideal may be seen in the preponderance of "quick and dirty" evaluations found throughout continuing education. Unfortunately, the efficiency of those practices is often not matched by their effectiveness.

Cost control is achieved most effectively by concentrating on high cost components. Evaluation is labor intensive. Direct salary and indirect time costs comprise the bulk of expense for most evaluations. More expense may be trimmed by cutting 10 percent of salary costs rather than 50 percent of postage costs for most evaluations. If more efficient ways can be found to plan evaluations, develop instruments, interpret findings, and write reports, the fixed costs of labor intensive activities can be significantly reduced. Some suggestions include designing systematic procedures for repeated use across several evaluations, purchasing existing materials wherever possible to reduce developmental costs, and developing simple guidelines to follow for data analysis and report writing. Worthy examples are provided in the *Program Evaluation Kit* (Morris, 1978).

Thoughtful reduction of costs should center on three areas.

Given a set of evaluation objectives, a search for savings through more efficient alternative strategies and activities is warranted. Substituting smaller sample sizes or using telephone interviews instead of personal visits are examples. Also, the underlying issues of interpretation and proof can be examined. Lesser potential for interpretation and lesser degrees of proof may be acceptable. Less information can be collected, indirect evidence can be substituted for direct evidence, or research designs with fewer observations and fewer control groups can be chosen. Given a limited budget, it is often more appropriate to change the objectives for evaluation as a third possibility. It is better to conduct an evaluation of acceptable quality than one that is not feasible to conduct well within the budget.

costs and benefits

Cost-benefit analysis is sometimes used to evaluate programs, but its use to evaluate evaluation has been limited. There is an absence of experience in using cost-benefit analysis with evaluation as its focus. In a double-loop sense, the costs of doing cost-benefit analysis to determine if evaluation should be done may not be warranted since they may absorb the funds available for evaluation itself. Nevertheless, decision makers in continuing education need procedures to assess the tangible and intangible benefits of evaluation.

Costs of evaluation can be objectively estimated using existing administrative practices in continuing education, but estimation of benefits remains subjective and intangible. Intuitively, more appears to be at stake for evaluations of larger, more expensive programs, but precise estimates of benefit are not generally attempted. Benefits may be less than costs in smaller programs because basic fixed costs comprise a greater proportion of total evaluation costs for smaller evaluations. For short programs where expected changes will be minimal there may be little benefit from evaluation. Where evaluation findings have no chance of affecting either the administrator's belief about program effectiveness or the decisions to be made about the program, there may be little benefit from evaluation. Those intuitive judgments about benefits need to be replaced with systematic estimates including some broadly based judgments about economic, political, and public relations components of benefit. The procedures exist in other fields where cost-benefit analysis is commonly used, and there are evident needs for their use in continuing education. Borrowing and modifying such procedures can be justified as a task for the future.

conclusions

When total costs are considered there are few bargains in evaluation. The most to be hoped for is fair value for time and resources spent. Any decision maker hoping for a $500 solution to a $1000 evaluation problem is likely to be disappointed. All evaluations are not expensive, however. Many need only minimal resources, given their purposes. Evaluation is desirable when benefits, estimated as well as possible, outweigh costs. When all possible ways to reduce costs have been exhausted and benefits of evaluation remain below costs, evaluation cannot be recommended.

Evaluation has been treated in continuing education literature as something that should be done for all programs as part of the normal program development process. However, there is a discrepancy between that view and its application in the field. Cost-effectiveness may help explain the discrepancy, and administrators should support development of techniques to determine whether or not impact evaluations should be conducted for specific programs.

references

Campbell, D. T., and Stanley, J. C. *Experimental and Quasi-Experimental Designs for Research.* Chicago: Rand McNally, 1966.

Grotelueschen, A. D., and others. *An Evaluation Planner.* Urbana: University of Illinois at Urbana-Champaign, Office for the Study of Continuing Professional Education, 1974.

Kirkpatrick, D. "Evaluating Training Programs: Evidence Vs. Proof." *Training and Development Journal,* 1977, *31* (11), 9–12.

Morris, L. L. (Ed.). *Program Evaluation Kit.* Beverly Hills, Calif.: Sage, 1978.

Popham, W. J. *Educational Evaluation.* Englewood Cliffs, N.J.: Prentice-Hall, 1975.

Stake, R. E. "The Countenance of Educational Evaluation." *Teachers College Record,* 1967, *68,* 523–540.

Stufflebeam, D. L. "A Conceptualization of Evaluation." AERA Tape Series on Educational Research, Audiotape. Washington, D.C.: American Educational Research Association, 1973.

Warr, P., Bird, M., and Rackham, N. *Evaluation of Management Training.* London: Gower Press, 1970.

Dale Rusnell is an assistant professor, Department of Adult Education, University of British Columbia. His primary interests relate to training in business and industry.

The general field of educational evaluation contains many
concepts, reports, and references that can be useful to
continuing education evaluators.

issues in assessing
educational impact

douglas d. sjogren

The purposes of this chapter are to identify some of the most important
issues in assessing impact of continuing education and to help the reader
become familiar with the thinking of several evaluation methodologists
on the issues. I am using the term "impact" to refer to outcomes or
effects of a continuing education activity that are assessed beyond the
instructional program. For a specific continuing education course, impact might be assessed in terms of the application of knowledge or use of
a skill learned in the course. For ongoing programs, such as an entire
Cooperative Extension Service program area, outcomes may be assessed
as a cumulative impact on work or life style.

    Using the formative-summative evaluation distinction that was
first defined by Scriven (1967), impact assessment and evaluation is generally of the summative type in that it is concerned with whether the
activity has achieved or is achieving the ultimate purpose. However, the
results of impact evaluation can often be used formatively, if the results
indicate that program objectives are not being met and program modifi-
cations are suggested.

For many continuing education activities, assessing impact is difficult to do. This situation is not unique to continuing education, however. It is pervasive in all of education, in fact, in all social endeavors. Most educational programs have either explicit or implicit goals that are rather broad, general statements of ultimate purpose. Specific objectives are derived from the goals and the specific objectives become the expected immediate outcomes of specific activities. The expectation is, of course, that if the objectives are attained the goals will be reached. Unfortunately, the direct relationship between the objectives and the goals is not usually well-supported by empirical evidence. There are many reasons for this lack of empirical evidence, some of which will be discussed below. It is important to recognize, however, that evaluation methodologists generally have stressed assessment of attainment of objectives rather than of goals when dealing with impact assessment. Worthen and Sanders (1973) and Tyler (1969) provide general summaries on evaluation methodology.

The methodological difficulties and the high cost are probably the main reasons for the relatively small number of impact studies done in education. There are relatively few examples of impact studies in the educational literature. Three of the more well-known studies are the eight-year study (Smith and Tyler, 1942), Project Talent (Flanagan, 1971), and the National Longitudinal Study of the High School Class of 1972 (Peng, Stafford, and Talbert, 1977). Also in recent years there have been some economic impact studies especially in vocational-technical education. An example of such a study is Kraft (1974).

issues

Assessment of impact is generally considered desirable because evidence that a program does or does not contribute to the achievement of individual or societal goals is useful for program support and modification. There are many issues that need consideration, however, in planning and conducting an impact assessment and evaluation.

Evaluation and Research. Evaluation and research activities often look alike, and they do overlap in the sense that both are a form of "disciplined inquiry" (Worthen and Sanders, 1973). They overlap in purpose, yet there is a distinction that should be kept in mind. Research has the purpose of identifying generalizable knowledge while evaluation has the purpose of determining the worth of something. In my experience, however, many persons involved in evaluation are very much concerned about generalization in the sense that they want to "prove" that their program is not only worthy, but the best. This approach unfortunately leads to a great amount of frustration because the "proof" is not attainable. Certainly the methods of science or disciplined inquiry are appropriate to evaluation, but use of the methods does not automatically make the effort a truly scientific study. Furthermore, as Scriven (1967) and Stake (1967) have both argued, evaluation is a judgmental process. Judgments are an important part of evaluation data, much more so than in research.

The distinction between evaluation and research is useful in planning for impact assessment in that the evaluation approach is less restrictive in terms of methods that yield acceptable and useful information. The fact that evaluation is a form of "disciplined inquiry" does indicate that the basic designs used in evaluation work are similar to the designs used in research. There are many books on research methods that define the basic designs that could be used in evaluation. One of the best sources is Kerlinger (1964).

Paradox of Evaluation. Glass (1975) wrote about the paradox of excellence which essentially described two contrasting points of view toward evaluation: (1) that it inhibits excellence; (2) that it stimulates excellence. The paradox might be related to time, that is, evaluations that occur too soon may be of more harm than help, but ultimately evaluation will be useful. This seems to apply in considering assessment of impact of continuing education. Especially with broad programs that are cumulative in effect it would seem that it would take time for much impact to occur. Thus, if assessed too quickly, the impact assessment would yield unfavorable results and cause a good program to be hurt. For example, how long was Cooperative Extension functioning until there was clear evidence of impact? Impact assessment should surely not occur until sufficient time has elapsed to permit an impact. There is a trade-off, however, that is dealt with in the next issue.

Context. Stufflebeam (1968) and Stake (1967) have both stressed the importance of considering program context in evaluation. Their emphasis has been on describing and understanding the contextual constraints that affect the functioning of the educational program. Context is also important in assessment of impact. Whether an impact is observed or not may depend on the context in which the assessment is made. There are multiple influences on individuals or organizations; which is to say that there are multiple causes for behavior. Thus a desired impact may not be observed because of other influences, or the impact may be observed but the main influence may not be the program. It is virtually impossible from a methodological viewpoint to attribute cause to a single program or activity. This is probably the major reason why evaluation is usually done on the basis of attainment of short-term objectives rather than long-term goals. Furthermore, as the assessment becomes increasingly removed from the event in terms of time, the causal link becomes more tenuous.

There is tremendous pressure on program administrators to provide impact evidence. The administrator should certainly attempt to provide such evidence, but also should recognize that contextual constraints generally limit the extent to which strong causal inferences can be made.

Power of Treatment. Charters and Jones (1973) discussed a problem in program evaluation in which they argued that often the program being evaluated was not sufficiently major to make impact likely. Methodologically this is the "power of treatment" issue. My observation is that often the expectations regarding power of treatment are unrealistically high, especially with short-term programs. The objectives of some two-day workshops sound like the workshop will rid the world of war, disease, pestilence, and famine. Any impact assessment certainly should be consistent with a realistic consideration of likely impacts.

Unit of Analysis. An important consideration in research design is to define the sampling frame and the organizational level at which the data will be analyzed. This is also of importance when considering impact assessment. At what level will the impact be observed: individual behavior, family patterns, or group performance? It is important for the planner of an impact assessment to define clearly the kind of impact expected at the appropriate level and to develop sampling and assessment procedures consistent with the definition.

Intended and Unintended Impact. Stake (1967) provided an extensive discussion of the importance of considering outcomes beside those that were specifically defined in the program goals and objectives. Scriven (1974) has further argued that in some circumstances program evaluation might be done on a goal-free basis. The Scriven argument is that the most important impacts of a program (positive or negative) may be independent of the stated purposes. If the evaluation is designed only to find out if the stated purposes are met, then some important impacts of the program may be ignored.

Associated with the idea of assessing intended and unintended impacts is the realization that a program may contribute to a large number of impacts. At times we are too constrained or unimaginative in defining or recognizing the many criteria that might be used in program evaluation. Metfessel and Michael (1967) identified a large number of criteria that might be used for school program evaluation. Darcy, Ballard, and Farley (1979) have defined a similar list for Vocational Education outcomes. While these references are not specific to continuing education, a reading of them will be useful for broadening thinking about possible impacts.

Measurement. In any assessment situation, a basic requirement is that the assessment procedure yields reliable and valid information. I argued in the previous paragraph that we often have a narrow perception of the possible impacts of a program. In a similar view, we also may have a narrow perception of the assessment procedures that are available.

An article by Sjogren (1970) provides a review of many assessment procedures used in evaluation. Webb and others (1966) is an excellent source for broadening one's perception of possible assessment procedures. Most research methods and educational measurement books contain information on construction of various assessment instruments. A research methods book by Tuckman (1978) is especially useful in this regard.

Standards. An important issue of concern in assessing impact is selection of a criterion for concluding that an impact was observed. If one plans the impact study while planning the program, then it is often possible to obtain baseline data that can be used for comparison. Even with baseline data, however, the standard for concluding that an impact occurred because there was a change from baseline assessment to impact assessment is elusive. Statistical procedures are often used to support the conclusion, but it is important to recognize that statistical significance does not necessarily mean importance. Forest and Marshall (1978) reported an interesting and promising panel approach for deciding on standards. It would seem that this approach is a practical and appropriate procedure for defining standards in many continuing education situations.

Meta-Evaluation. As both consumers and producers of evaluations, continuing education practitioners must be judges of the evaluation effort. To say that a program has been evaluated does not say much without consideration of whether the design and procedures were appropriate. Evaluation reports should be read critically, and the designer of an evaluation activity will benefit from a critique of the proposed

114

design. The process of evaluating evaluations is generally referred to as meta-evaluation. An article by Scriven (1969) provides useful ideas on this issue.

summary

Assessment of impact of continuing education activities is a complex problem with many issues bearing on the problem. Perhaps the overriding issue is that continuing education systems are parts of larger systems. Continuing education interacts with other components to not only produce impact but also in competition for resources. It is important that continuing education attempt to identify how it contributes to the system. These attempts will help our understanding of the unique role of continuing education for individuals and society. Increased understanding will also provide support for continuing education in its competition for resources.

references

Charters, W., and Jones, J. "On the Risk of Appraising Non-Events in Program Evaluation." *Educational Researcher,* 1973, *2* (11), 5–7.
Darcy, R., Ballard, K., and Farley, J. *Vocational Educations Outcomes.* Columbus, Ohio: The National Center for Research in Vocational Education, 1979.
Flanagan, J., and others. *Project Talent—Five Years After High School.* Palo Alto, Calif.: American Institutes for Research, 1971.
Forest, L., and Marshall, M. *Impact of Extension in Shawano County: Methodology.* Madison: University of Wisconsin-Extension, 1978.
Glass, G. "A Paradox about Excellence of Schools and People in Them." *Educational Researcher,* 1975, *4* (3), 9–13.
Kerlinger, F. *Foundations of Behavioral Research.* New York: Holt, Rinehart and Winston, 1964.
Kraft, R. "Cost-Effectiveness Analysis in Vocational-Technical Education." In R. Kraft, and others, *Four Evaluation Examples: Anthropological, Economic, Narrative, and Portrayed.* AERA Monograph Series on Curriculum Evaluation, No. 7. Chicago: Rand McNally, 1974.
Metfessel, N., and Michael W. "A Paradigm Involving Multiple Criterion Measures for the Evaluation of the Effectiveness of School Programs." *Education and Psychological Measurement,* 1967, *27,* 931–943.
Peng, S., Stafford, C., and Talbert, R. *National Longitudinal Study Review and Annotation of Study Reports.* Research Triangle Institute, N.C.: Center for Education Research and Evaluation, 1977.
Scriven, M. "The Methodology of Evaluation." In R. Tyler, R. Gagne, and M. Scriven (Eds.), *Perspectives of Curriculum Evaluation.* Chicago: Rand McNally, 1967.
Scriven, M. "An Introduction to Meta-Evaluation." *Educational Product Report,* 1969, *2* (5), 36–38.

Scriven, M. "Pros and Cons about Goal-Free Evaluation." In W. J. Popham (Ed.), *Evaluation in Education: Current Applications.* Berkeley, Calif.: McCutchan, 1974.

Sjogren, D. "Measurement Techniques in Evaluation." *Review of Educational Research,* 1970, *40* (2), 301–320.

Smith, E., and Tyler, R. *Appraising and Recording Student Progress.* New York: Harper and Bros., 1942.

Stake, R. "The Countenance of Educational Evaluation." *Teachers College Record,* 1967, *68* (7), 523–430.

Stufflebeam, D. *Evaluation as Enlightenment for Decision Making.* Columbus, Ohio: Ohio State University, Evaluation Center, 1968.

Tuckman, B. *Conducting Educational Research.* New York: Harcourt Brace Jovanovich, 1978.

Tyler, R. (Ed.). *Educational Evaluation—New Roles, New Means.* Chicago: National Society for the Study of Education, 1969.

Webb, E., and others. *Unobtrusive Measures: Nonreactive Research in the Social Sciences.* Chicago: Rand McNally, 1966.

Worthen, B., and Sanders, J. *Education Evaluation: Theory and Practice.* Worthington, Ohio: Charles A. Jones, 1973.

Douglas Sjogren is a professor in the Department of Education, Colorado State University, at Fort Collins. An educational psychologist, Sjogren has extensive experience in educational evaluation, especially with continuing education and vocational education programs.

*There is sufficient evidence from impact studies throughout
the field to conclude that continuing education can have
an impact on evaluation. The challenge is to increase the
proportion of programs that do so and to develop more
efficient procedures to assess impact.*

conclusions about
impact evaluation

alan b. knox

This book has reviewed issues, approaches, and findings regarding continuing education impact evaluation. The focus has been on follow-up
studies and other efforts to assess program impact in the form of improved performance and other societal benefits. The evidence is impressive that continuing education programs can have a major impact on
performance. However, such benefits are not automatic and they are not
easily assessed. This final chapter reviews the major conclusions about
impact evaluation.

The preceding chapters summarize and refer to an impressive
number of evaluation and research studies that report evidence of impact of continuing education activities on subsequent performance by
participants. The evaluation projects studied various types of program
formats and clientele groups across most segments of the field. It should
be noted, however, that it is not known what proportion of all continuing
education programs has been evaluated regarding impact, or even how
representative these impact evaluation *reports* are of all studies that have
been conducted. The careful search entailed in the preparation of this

book indicates that many of the more rigorous impact studies have been identified. The conclusion that all continuing education programs have a major impact on subsequent performance of participants is clearly not warranted. However, the conclusion that some programs do have an impact is irrefutable. There is sufficient evidence of benefits that practitioners throughout the field should have pride and optimism about what they *can* accomplish. Thus, one major conclusion is that practitioners have many impact studies that they can review and refer to in response to those who question whether continuing education can make a difference. In general, well-designed continuing education programs under favorable circumstances can have an impact on performance and results that can be convincingly documented by well-designed impact evaluation studies.

This leads to a consideration of the conditions under which continuing education programs are likely to have an impact. This issue is the focus of the professional literature on continuing education program development. Some programs are not as well designed as they might be, and program evaluation to help planners recognize concepts and practices that could help them conduct more effective programs would make a useful contribution. The purpose of this book was not to critique the effectiveness of procedures to plan and conduct programs, but instead to review findings about impact and procedures to assess it. However, two general program characteristics can be identified that are likely to contribute to impact. One is that the program deals directly with specific and achievable changes in performance that are important to the adult learner, are amenable to educational influence, and that can be readily documented. The second is that the type and amount of educational intervention is likely to bring about the desired change in performance. This includes attention to various forms of education related to knowledge, skill, and attitude as well as multiple influences on stability and change in performance. In some continuing education programs, the disparity between grandiose expectations and an anemic intervention is so great that a serious effort to assess impact would be laughable. Even when these two conditions are met (achievable change, reasonable intervention) it is difficult to conduct an impact study likely to prove the extent and types of benefits attributable to the program and not to other influences.

Assessment of the impact of continuing education participation on improved performance by the learners as they apply their increased proficiency in family, work, and community, often entails attention to organizational change as well as personal change. Those who seek to conduct conclusive impact studies will require all they can borrow from the methodological literature of educational evaluation and applied research in the social and behavioral sciences, and then some. Even when experimental studies are feasible, the term "intervening variables" fails to convey the power of these other influences to confound efforts to attribute benefits to an educational program in a causal way. Voluntary participation makes it likely that influences on initial participation also affect application of what is learned. Influences from ongoing adult life that are concurrent with the educational program can nullify or redouble program impact in many and subtle ways. It is difficult to marshal support sufficient to rigorously assess the impact of a continuing education program under these circumstances. In many instances, the benefits of doing so would not be worth the costs. Practitioners who seek to conduct an impact evaluation are well advised to include personnel in the project who are highly proficient in the use of impact evaluation procedures. Review of full reports for some of the impact studies identified in this book could contribute to sound planning. Most of the reports are readily available.

As meager as the number of available continuing education impact evaluation reports seem to be, they stand up well when compared with the very few impact evaluations of preparatory education application beyond the educational program, and even of the impact of performance by practitioners in the helping professions on the people they intend to benefit. Even in those segments of the field of continuing education in which there has been longstanding attention to results, such as in the Cooperative Extension Service and in educational programs employers provide for their employees, there are fewer published impact studies than might be expected.

Part-time and short-term continuing education programs for adults provide unique opportunities to assess relationships between education and action. Continuing education programs typically have multiple benefits, several of which can usually be assessed in a specific impact study. Included are a personal sense of understanding or mastery, adoption of changed practices, economic benefits such as increased productivity, organizational survival, and various benefits for the larger society such as creativity and support of sound policies. The assessment of such changes and benefits can be based on self-reports, records, and ratings by peers and supervisors. Evidence of impact can be collected at one particular time, such as in a follow-up study, but it tends to be most convincing when there is some type of longitudinal or time series data to indicate the probable impact of the educational program on participants compared with data from similar adults who did not participate. Without some type of comparison or control group it is difficult, if not impossible, to conclude what changes are the result of the decision to participate, and what changes are the result of participation. The most convincing conclusions have emerged from studies that have used two or more sources of evidence for purposes of triangulation or cross validation.

This is one of the reasons why a fairly comprehensive framework is so useful for conducting impact studies. A study can only include a small portion of all of the potential variables, but it can increase the likelihood that the ones selected are important. Such a comprehensive framework focuses on major instances of information seeking and problem solving in which adults engage, which are most germane to the educational program to be evaluated. Such a framework also includes attention to the total system in which the adult functions, the main changes in performance in that system likely to be affected by the educational program, organizational and societal benefits likely to result from changes in performance, the main program processes likely to be associated with impact, and other influences likely to affect assumed impact. Consideration of such variables can help an evaluator design and conduct an impact study that is both desirable and feasible.

A desirable impact study results in a convincing report on the extent and types of benefits that resulted from a continuing education program, such as improved performance. It also gives some indication of program features that affect impact so that practitioners know what to preserve and strengthen. A feasible study has at least the potential to produce findings that are worth the costs of the evaluation. Manageable impact studies tend to be very selective. Few impact evaluations can carry the burden of all that is expected unless evaluators use other research and evaluation studies to develop instruments and procedures, and to provide generalizations to help interpret impact evaluation findings.

A major breakthrough in impact evaluation in each program area would occur as a result of major research studies to identify the extent and types of impact that continuing education programs typically have and to specify indexes of this impact that could be readily used to assess the probable impact of most continuing education programs in that program area. The research study would produce proof of impact and of the extent of association with the index. The index would then provide an efficient means of estimating impact. Many practitioners seem to be using expressions of participant satisfaction as such an index. However, there is mixed evidence of the association between satisfaction with the program and change in performance. Relative satisfaction with the program does seem to persist for months or even years, however. Convincing impact evaluation is clearly important for program improvement and especially justification. Thus, meta-evaluation should receive high priority as a means of increasing the efficiency and effectiveness of impact evaluations.

Alan B. Knox has long been engaged in evaluation efforts to improve and justify continuing education programs. He has spent years as a practitioner helping to plan and evaluate programs, and has written extensively on program evaluation.

index